The Samaritans in the '70s

Pamela
with love from
Shad 1/1.

The Samaritans in the '70s

to befriend the suicidal and despairing

Edited with an Introduction by
CHAD VARAH

Constable London

First published in Great Britain 1973
by Constable and Company Ltd
10 Orange Street London WC2H 7EG

Copyright © 1973 by The Samaritans

ISBN 0 09 458330 7 (cloth)
0 09 459260 8 (paper)

1st edition 1965
2nd revised edition 1973

Set in Monotype Bembo
Printed in Great Britain by The Anchor Press Ltd,
and bound by Wm. Brendon & Son Ltd, both of Tiptree, Essex

I saw one fallen in the sand, half sitting, half lying upon his hands. This was a religious mendicant, some miserable derwish in his clouted beggar's cloak, who groaned in extremity, holding forth his hands like eagles' claws to man's pity. Last in the long train, we went also marching by him. His beggar's scrip, full of broken morsels, fallen from his neck, was poured out before him. The wretch lamented to the slow moving lines of the Mecca-bound pilgrimage: the many had passed on, and doubtless as they saw his dying, hoped inwardly the like evil ending might not be their own. Some charitable serving men, Damascenes, in our company stepped aside to him; *ana meyet*, sobbed the derwish, I am a dying man. One then of our crew, he was also my servant, a valiant outlaw, no holy-tongue man but of human deeds, with a manly heartening word, couched by an empty camel, and with a spring of his stalwart arms, lifted and set him fairly upon the pack saddle. The dying derwish gave a weak cry much like a child, and hastily they raised the camel under him and gathered his bag of scattered victuals and reached it to him, who sat all feeble murmuring thankfulness, and trembling yet for fear. There is no ambulance service with the barbarous pilgrim army; and all charity is cold, in the great and terrible wilderness, of that wayworn suffering multitude.

From *Arabia Deserta*
by Charles M. Doughty

This book is dedicated to all those who make or find life worth living by giving and receiving love – the Samaritans and those whom they help

Contents

Contents

Contents

Introduction

Chad Varah

The Samaritans are about 17,000 men and women who dedicate a generous part of their leisure time to the prevention of suicide by alleviating human loneliness, misery and despair. Theirs are the quiet, unhurried voices which, at any hour of the day or night, any day of the year, answer one of over 125 emergency telephones with the words, 'The Samaritans – can I help you?' Because of their devotion to their chosen task, and their loving concern for those who are at the end of their tether and thought nobody cared, 5,000 human beings are alive who might otherwise be dead. Thousands more live more happily and hopefully because of the friendship of The Samaritans. Some of them were once themselves in the position of feeling they could not go on but found that a Samaritan emergency telephone was their lifeline.

In ever increasing numbers of centres at home and overseas, Samaritans are turning up regularly on duty, manning the telephones, receiving those who call in person, spending countless hours in patient and usually undramatic befriending of people who often have no one else to turn to, and sometimes, more dramatically, speeding to the scene of someone's last struggle with despair. They do not appear on television, and their names are not reported on the radio or in the Press; they receive no praise and look for no thanks; and they are blissfully unaware that they are the salt of the earth. They create oases of humanity in the desert of man's selfishness and indifference, and only when their attitude is adopted by the greater part of the population will the sickness of our society be healed.

How the Samaritans began

Whenever I hear myself referred to as the Founder of The Samaritans, I want to protest: 'I didn't found them – I didn't even *find* most of them. The first of them found *me*, and without them The Samaritans would not exist.' I chose the name, not only because the parable of the Good Samaritan inspires our work, but because it implies a collection of *people*, in each of whom the purpose of the fellowship is to be fulfilled. A 'Suicide Prevention Centre' would be a *place*; a 'Lifeline' a *thing*; 'Dial aid' a nice palindromic slogan; whilst a 'Society for the Prevention of Suicide' would have conjured up the idea of officials and committees and an organisation rather than a fellowship of compassionate people any one of whom could be relied upon not to pass by on the other side. A person who is in despair and tempted to take his own life would not risk being told, 'I will put your application before our Board, which meets on Wednesday week.' He needs a compassionate fellow human being to whom he can say, 'Will *you* help me? Now?' Each Samaritan invites this appeal. Naturally, there has to be an organisation if a Samaritan is always to be available however many people seek help at once, and if various kinds of professional help are also to be provided; but the organisation exists in order to put the right person in the right place at the right time.

It all began with an offer of personal help. When I made it known in the Press that from 2 November 1953 people contemplating suicide were invited to telephone me at MANsion House 9000, I did not think of myself as founding an organisation, still less a world movement, as it has now become. It was a very small act of obedience on my part and I never dreamt what extensive use God and man would be able to make of it. Indeed, I hardly looked ahead at all: if I had known what I was letting myself in for in the first few years, I do not know whether I should have dared to make that rash offer. I have a tendency to act on impulse, and whilst sometimes I have had cause to regret this, at other times I have been glad eventually that I landed myself in a position that scared me, but in which it was easier to go on than to turn back. This was how I overcame a certain timidity left by a sickly, weedy childhood.

When I read, in the summer of 1953, that there were three suicides a day in Greater London, in spite of our extensive medical and social services, I thought something ought to be done about it – and if I had had any sense, I should have written to *The Times* and said so. Instead, I asked myself whether I ought not to do something about it. I suppose this comes partly from having been blessed with parents who were accustomed to do what they conceived to be their duty rather than to wonder vaguely why the Government did not do something, and partly through being the eldest of nine children, which leads one to feel responsible for others and to think one ought to look after them when necessary. I know one has to be on the watch against being overprotective or doing things for people which it would be better if they did themselves, but one cannot care about people without feeling responsible for them in trouble, and one just has to beware that a helping hand does not become interference.

Throughout my ministry, I had always been more interested in counselling than in other kinds of parochial work. I started giving pastoral preparation for marriage, including sexual instruction, to young couples whilst I was still an unmarried deacon. I was happiest when dealing with people one by one, in a sick-room or hospital, in my study or the confessional, by a coffin or in a condemned cell; and, apart from taking services, I felt I was being a priest when I was doing this rather than when I was keeping the parochial machinery grinding on. I felt I had not been ordained in order to spend seven-eighths of my time as a bored administrator and unsuccessful commercial traveller, and although I was happy looking after a congregation of 100 wonderful people in a parish of 10,000 in South London, with the chaplaincy of a hospital thrown in, the idea of reversing these proportions and being able to spend seven-eighths of my time being a priest (as I understood this) appeared to me more a yielding to inclination than any sort of sacrifice. I have always believed that vocation is not usually a matter of the Archangel Gabriel yelling clear instructions at one through a celestial megaphone, but more a matter of God working His will by insinuating promptings into our circumstances and interests and inclinations, not because inclinations cannot be temptations, but because we mostly do best what we have some aptitude for and like doing. In other words, God's 'call' is a challenge to us to find out what we are *for*. I did not find out what I was for until I was forty-two.

The idea then of giving all my time to those with whom life has dealt so harshly that they are not sure they want to go on with it appealed to me. 'Three suicides a day in

Greater London' did not appear to me to be simply statistics, but desolate people whom I could imagine dying miserably in lonely rooms. That is one of the penalties of being a visualiser – a freakish condition I inherited from my mother. A visualiser has a vivid visual imagination, and sees pictures in his mind's eye in 3D and in colour. It was because of this that I was staff script-writer visualiser for *Eagle* and *Girl* for twelve years, and I remember that when I was told one day that each copy of *Eagle* was read by three and a quarter boys, I shuddered at the grisly picture of a bloodstained quarter of a boy holding *Eagle* in his only hand and reading it with half an eye. The faculty makes it very painful reading about atrocities and disasters in newspapers, and I was haunted by the pictures of a different person every eight hours dying by his or her own hand in the city in which I lived.

Because my early training was scientific, a number of pertinent questions posed themselves in my mind. What sort of people were behind these dreadful statistics? Were they all mentally ill? Did they need psychiatry? If so, why did they not apply for it? Or if they did, why did it not save them? Could not some be helped by professional social workers? If so, why did they not apply to these? Doubtless, great numbers of potential suicides were helped by psychiatrists and other doctors, by social workers, and by clergymen and ministers, but there were still three a day in London who died by their own hands. What, if anything, could have saved them? In addition to the suicidal acts which led to death, there were perhaps ten times as many where the act was not fatal. Was it necessary for all of these to harm themselves or even endanger their lives in order to draw attention to their plight, or might they be willing to accept help if it were available without recourse to such desperate measures?

There were some clues to the answers to these questions.

A great many people have a fear of psychiatry and in particular of mental hospitals, and this fear is often strongest in those who have need of such services. Many people who need psychiatry are brought to it only by the intervention of anxious relatives or friends. What of those who have neither?

Coroners' verdicts nearly always assumed that a person who had committed suicide was mentally ill at the time. Was this assumption justified, or was it a merciful fiction allowing the remains to be buried in consecrated ground, thus avoiding further distress to already grieved relatives? People close to the deceased, often intelligent observers, were sometimes doubtful whether the emotional disturbance which led to the suicidal act was of the nature of a mental illness treatable by psychiatry. Subsequent research into this question has shown that 30 per cent of those who do commit suicide have had psychiatric treatment, and it is estimated that half as many again ought to have had such treatment. Ignoring the fact that the 30 per cent died in spite of the treatment they had had, this still leaves 55 per cent, a majority, of whom it appeared true to say that they required some kind of attention other than psychiatric treatment, and the 45 per cent who *were* psychiatric cases needed some other kind of ministration in addition to medical help.

The need for counselling

What kind of help was required, either instead of or in addition to psychiatry? Was it possible that non-medical counselling might save at least some of those contemplating suicide?

In the summer of 1953, I had an opportunity to discover how useful, in some cases, such counselling could be. I had written an article for a magazine called *Picture Post*, giving what I believed to be an enlightened, Christian philosophy of sex. This may well have been the beginning of the permissive society as far as this stands for less repressive attitudes to the sexual behaviour of others. The correspondence which this article provoked kept me busy for several weeks, almost all the letters being from people who had been troubled, often for years, about some sexual problem, and had not found anyone in whom they felt they could confide without fear of condemnation. Exactly a hundred of these letters arrived the day after the publication of the article, and out of these, 14 were written by people who appeared to be in such agony of mind about their sexual problems that they were on the verge of suicide. The remarkable thing was that only one of these needed to be referred to a psychiatrist: the other 13 (one of whom had in the past had some psychiatric attention) were able to be helped, apparently satisfactorily, by straightforward counselling, in most cases without explicit religious content.

It is impossible to guess how many of the remaining 86 out of these first 100 correspondents might have become suicidal if they had not found someone with whom to discuss their problems acceptably. Out of a total of 235 persons who wrote as a result of that article, 2 dozen appeared to be suicidal, 3 of whom I advised to seek medical help. It is interesting that this proportion, 1 in 8, has continued to be roughly the proportion of the serious cases coming to The Samaritans referred for psychiatric treatment. I am not, of course, suggesting that only $12\frac{1}{2}$ per cent of potential suicides need psychiatry more urgently than they need anything else: the potential suicides who seek the help of The Samaritans are clearly not typical of the whole range of potential suicides, and it is not surprising that the majority of those who need psychiatry seek it without coming to The Samaritans first.

MAN 9000

Once I was reasonably certain that non-medical counselling had *some* contribution to make, however small, towards the prevention of suicide, I felt a clear duty to take steps to try to provide this for all who might be persuaded to apply for it. But how was such counselling to be made available, and its existence brought to the attention of those who might benefit from it? There was no way of knowing who the potential suicides were, so the only way they could be informed of the existence of an emergency service specially for them was by informing everybody; and the only practical way of informing everybody was through the good offices of the Press (and later of radio and television).

The first necessity, however, was time to operate such a service, a base from which to operate, and an income on which to live while doing it. A church in the City of London, where there are hardly any parochial responsibilities because of the lack of resident population, was the obvious answer. Out of the blue I received the offer of the Lord Mayor's Parish Church of St Stephen Walbrook, from the Patrons, the Worshipful Company of Grocers, who subsequently appointed me Rector because, having had my scheme explained to them, they wished the experiment to be tried. (Eleven years later, the Worshipful Company showed their satisfaction with the results of that experiment by paying the cost of the conversion of the crypt of the church into premises from which The Samaritans could continue to operate, whoever might subsequently hold the position of Rector. I named this crypt 'Grocers' Gift').

The idea of an emergency service automatically brought to mind the telephone, on the dial of which in those days appeared the words: 'Emergency calls – for police, fire, ambulance DIAL 999'. Citizens have long been accustomed to make for the telephone in an emergency, but the 999 system did not cater for those whose emergency was not that their house had been burgled or caught fire, or they themselves physically injured in some accident, but that they were in such despair that they were contemplating self-destruction. There seemed no good reason why there should not be a fourth emergency service, for potential suicides; but in the experimental stage it could clearly not be a nationwide addition to the 999 system. We now know that the intervention of an operator asking 'Which service, please?' would make it unsuitable for *all* calls to be via 999, though now we are nearly a nationwide network I don't see why those who wish should not dial 999 and ask for us.

I knew the telephone at St Stephen Walbrook must be on the Mansion House exchange, so either 9999 or 9000 would be sufficiently reminiscent of 999 for the proposed pilot emergency number. In 1953 the repair of the church after its severe damage in the blitz was almost complete and the contractors had had the telephone reconnected. It was covered with dust when I used it to enquire whether the number could be changed to MANsion House 9000. The operator replied that someone would be certain already to have such a desirable number, but she would make enquiries if I would tell her the number I was speaking from. I wiped the dust from the dial, and told her not to bother: St Stephen Walbrook already had the coveted number.

There was now a willing man with a base and an income and an emergency telephone with an easily memorised number. All that was required was for the Press to make that number widely known and for me to try to cope with what happened as a result. I had for six years had to earn my living in Fleet Street because my income was only sufficient to pay my secretary, so I had no difficulty in interesting the Press in such a 'human interest story' as the provision of an emergency telephone for potential suicides, and thousands of pounds' worth of free publicity for the scheme was willingly given, not only in the early days when it was 'news', but regularly over the years.

As soon as MANsion House 9000 was publicised, it began to be used, and mostly by people who could benefit to some extent from the counselling offered. Two things quickly became clear. First, that for many callers the telephone was only a convenient means of emergency contact requiring a minimum of effort and allowing anonymity to be maintained until confidence had been established, when in most cases the client wished to come for a face-to-face interview. Secondly, that no man, however devoted and efficient his secretary, could possibly meet the need of all the people who sought help, even when the service was new and the majority of potential clients had never heard of it. It was by no means unusual in those early days for me to have a succession of 11 one-hour interviews with old and new clients, constantly interrupted by telephone calls, with no time to go out for meals or even to do things for clients such as write letters or make telephone calls.

Fortunately, however, the publicity attracted offers of help as well as clients. Some of these offers turned out to be from people *needing* help, some from cranks, and some from would-be Lady Bountifuls or evangelisers, but there were one or two from professionals willing to help by having clients referred to them, and some from good-hearted people who genuinely wanted to help humbly in any way they could.

The first volunteers

It was by no means clear in what way good-hearted, un-qualified, 'ordinary' people could help potential suicides, except indirectly by ministering to, and running errands for, me while I tried to cope single-handed with the results of a very rash offer. It was they, not I, who discovered how they could help. They turned up regularly, and sat around in the outer vestry while I interviewed clients in the inner vestry, and, being the type of people they were, they did not allow clients waiting their turn to twiddle their thumbs, sit staring vacantly into space, or sob quietly in a corner, unless this was what the client wanted to do. The lay volunteers engaged the clients in conversation, plied them with coffee and cigarettes, and generally made them feel at home.

Three things began to happen whose significance was not immediately noticed. First, counselling began to go much better. Clients were not merely free of the exasperation which comes from long and tedious waiting, but were in a calmly receptive state of mind and had had their confidence in me, as the person doing the counselling, enormously built up. Secondly, a proportion of the clients went away happily without having had any counselling at all, having found all that they needed in the ministrations of the lay volunteers. This seemed to apply particularly to clients who on arrival had proclaimed in no uncertain terms that they wanted to see the Rector personally and were not going to be fobbed off with anybody else. Thirdly, the failures of my counselling were almost always picked up by the volunteers as the client passed through the outer vestry on the way out. The majority of these clients were psychotic, and therefore not amenable to counselling, but in a great number of cases were able to appreciate kindly interest and to benefit from the supportive friendship of volunteers who were determined to do something useful and were not afraid of making the situation worse, because it clearly could not be worse. Like the cheerful ward maid who makes friends with a patient in the closed ward of a mental hospital, blissfully ignorant of the fact that he is the most dangerous patient they have ever had, these volunteers were angels who rushed in where fools fear to tread.

They were not all equally good, of course, and some fell by the wayside, but the best of them remained for years and it is to them rather than to myself that The Samaritans owes its origin. The *Daily Mirror* had published a story under the optimistic headline 'Samaritan Priest Will Save Suicides': it was only a few months before it became evident that the word 'Samaritan' needed to be put in the plural, and the word 'Priest' dropped. From that moment (early in 1954) the original concept of a non-medical (but still professional) counselling service was abandoned. Its place was taken by the concept of a befriending service by lay volunteers. These were selected by, and operated under the supervision of, someone who was capable of supplementing their efforts by counselling the clients or by referring them for treatment when necessary, but who would never again pick up the emergency telephone or receive a client on arrival if there were a Samaritan available to do this.

Befriending

Befriending, the distinguishing mark and characteristic activity of The Samaritans, had been discovered by the volunteers doing it and by me noticing and encouraging them to do more and more. I also became aware that although I wasn't as good at it as they were, some of my own most surprising and heartening results had come from dealings with clients that were examples of befriending rather than counselling.

There are many examples of the volunteers' befriending effecting what neither treatment nor counselling can achieve. A woman whose diagnosis was paranoid schizophrenia was discharged from hospital when there was no further improvement in her condition but she was judged not to be dangerous. Her husband would not have her back (we have had many such cases, some involving another woman and some not – I will not say which this was, or when, lest one of them should imagine she can identify herself, and then perhaps start thinking other people could). She was very lonely, and unlikely to be able to make friends because she was a great bore and also very suspicious and touchy. She came to us for help in getting a job – one of a great number whose presenting problem is not their main one. She was at that time quite unemployable, and if we had persuaded anyone to take her on they would never have helped us in this way again. The muddle she made of the occasional jobs she found for herself was fantastic; doubtless the firms concerned could afford it, but it was not doing *her* any good (except financially) to keep getting the sack with wages in lieu of notice. She was given a very patient and assiduous befriender, who spent countless hours with her over a period of years. There were many ups and downs, and at no stage could one speak of a 'cure', but the woman was able sometimes to hold down simple jobs for reasonable periods, and her life was much happier and her mental state improved. I could not have done what that befriender did – and not only because I have not as much time available.

Another case where befriending came to the rescue when all else failed was that of a man suffering from a severe depressive illness who flatly refused to see a doctor even though he agreed with me that only medical treatment could cure his depression. We have had hundreds of these. There were some indications that he had heard gruesome and misleading stories about electroplexy from a neighbour who knew someone who had had it; he called it 'shock treatment', though there is no shock; she called it 'ECT', which is short for 'electro-convulsive therapy', though most of the convulsive effect is nowadays avoided by relaxant drugs. He stated that 'over his dead body' would it be done to him. I told him it was for a doctor to decide what kind of treatment was necessary, and that without treatment there might be a dead body on which no one would waste electricity or anti-depressant drugs. After an hour's debate, he agreed that treatment would not hurt him and would relieve his depression; and added that he would not have it at any price. He reminded me that I had stated 'In The Paper' that clients were as free to go as they were to come, and that if after talking with us they still wanted to commit suicide, we would make no effort to prevent them by force. I agreed that this was so, and asked if he would like a Samaritan to drive him home. I will not say whether or not he was the man who for some reason I never discovered was carrying an enormously heavy sewing-machine with him, but he accepted the lift, and I briefed the person I had chosen to be his befriender. This Samaritan never made any reference to treatment or to depression or to me, but concentrated on making friends with the client, who some weeks later (including a couple of anxious occasions when his friend sat up all night with him) asked to be taken to the doctor because he felt he ought not to go on being 'such a burden' to his friend. (This client *did* have electroplexy and it cured him in about three weeks.)

Still another example of befriending being the real need was that of a young man who was painfully shy, and who wondered whether he might be homosexual since he never dared to address a girl and was tongue-tied if one addressed him. His only sexual experience (apart from standard adolescent masturbation, which, thanks to a wise clergyman who took his confirmation class, did not bother him) was years before, with another boy at school, who took the initiative. Such clients normally have at least a little counselling, but this one got swept into befriending at a busy period and by the time we got round to arranging it, it was clear he did not need it. His befriender refused to regard the problem as one of homosexuality, on the ground that the young man was equally shy with both sexes, and treated it simply as a problem of loneliness arising from lack of confidence (though if any complications had arisen he would of course have reported this, and some counselling would have been arranged). The befriender took the client with him to all sorts of functions where young people of both sexes were to be found, drew him out, saw to it that he was included in any conversation, made openings for him to tell an anecdote which the befriender had previously extracted from him and found entertaining; and so on. After a few weeks of this the client really began to hold his own in company, though he would never, mercifully, become 'the life and soul of the party'. A few months later, the client had found a girl friend, and the Samaritan withdrew, having been instrumental in completely transforming the client's life. It was typical that when this volunteer was given a small pat on the back – a thing we rarely do – he muttered that he had not done anything, really. Nor had he: except be a Samaritan, meeting the client's simple need.

All these befrienders were content to be members of a

body of lay people, who, like the Samaritan in the parable, are moved with compassion by the desperate plight of their fellow men and women, and who, lacking professional qualifications or competence, offer themselves and what they have to give, namely their personal concern, their time, attention and friendship. Samaritans come in all shapes and sizes, of all ages and both sexes, from all kinds of background, with all kinds of interests; and in a big enough collection to man an emergency telephone 24 hours a day; so there is sufficient variety to 'match' any client who comes looking for a real friend. The Samaritan listens, accepts, cares; and this can make all the difference between life and death for those who feel that no one has time for them, that they are rejected, and that nobody cares.

The Samaritans are all inspired by the same spirit. Even the most convinced unbeliever in the supernatural talks about 'spirit'. It is not necessary to believe in the Holy Spirit to use expressions like, 'There is a good spirit in this school, office, or scout troop.' It is not necessary to believe in a Personal Devil to use expressions like, 'There was a bad spirit in the meeting, community, or mob.' Whether one's thinking is theological or anti-theological, and whether one's attempts to formulate one's beliefs and a philosophy on which they rest make sense or not, it is an undeniable fact that there are movements or tendencies which affect people who are widely separated from one another, so that ideas appear to be born or to meet an enthusiastic response in many different places at about the same time.

It happens that the idea of an emergency telephone service for potential suicides started in my mind, but other minds all over the world were open to the idea and only had to hear of my London experiment to know at once that this was what they had been groping after. In addition, all over the world there are people who are contracting out of the 'rat race' and looking for some way of serving their fellow human beings in a spirit of neighbourly kindliness. However powerful may be the hold of a selfish and materialistic spirit which expresses itself in the slogan, 'I'm all right, Jack', not everyone has succumbed to this. In every street, if one could find them, are one or two people who are natural Samaritans; who cannot pass by on the other side like the Priest and the Levite, and are not afraid of being involved.

In every age there have been some people who were, in the original sense of the word, 'charitable'. In previous centuries most 'good works' have been done by people of this kind. In our day, the State has taken over more and more the responsibility for the welfare of its citizens, and this is a right and necessary development; but it has left many men and women of goodwill with a feeling of frustration, because there is so little that they can do for others which can compare with what professionally trained people can accomplish. To such people, The Samaritans, and other organisations which utilise the services of untrained volunteers, come as a godsend. To be able to make all the difference in the world to another human being is to find one's real self. People have grown accustomed to thinking of 'rescue' as something confined to doctors, ambulance men, firemen, lifeboat men, pit rescue squads and other specialised occupations – only by an unlikely chance would an ordinary citizen find himself in the position of being able to save a human life. Even if he *did* find himself in such a situation, he fears he would lack the skill or presence of mind to be able to intervene effectively. A child is drowning in the canal, and he has never learnt to swim; the victim of a motor accident is bleeding to death, and he cannot remember where the pressure points are; he wants to get someone out of a smoke-filled room, and does not know there is breathable air near the floor.

The person who does not *know* may fail in the rescue, or make the situation worse, or add himself to the number needing to be rescued. He will mostly be well advised to run and summon someone who is competent to cope with the particular situation.

Selection and preparation of volunteers

The beauty of The Samaritans as an opportunity for life-saving service is that by its very nature it does not require difficult skills: it simply requires a particular type of person. Friends may be good, bad or indifferent, and so may neighbours; and the good ones are good because of what they are, not because of particular technical skills. Certain skills may make a person more *useful*: if the couple next door consist of a handyman who can mend anything and a woman who is good at all kinds of domestic emergencies, this will increase their usefulness in a particular kind of crisis, but unless they are neighbourly people, liking to be of service, they might as well be hamhanded and stupid for all the good it will do for those next door. Since the essence of neighbourliness is kindness and interest rather than the ability to do jobs for which one would normally have to pay, a good neighbour may be totally unskilled and yet add greatly to life's contentment.

The Samaritan volunteer is accepted into the organisation not because he knows how to cope with someone who has taken an overdose, nor because of his experience in getting people down off roofs and window-ledges from which they threaten to jump. He (or she) is chosen not for any particular abilities (useful though these may be, and some volunteers have them), but for those human qualities that make a good friend, a good neighbour, a good person to have with you when you are in trouble. It is not so much by what he does, but by *being* his own patient, tolerant, interested self, that the Samaritan helps clients most. Someone can usually be found to do the things that require particular knowledge or abilities, and the Samaritan is prepared to go to endless trouble about this, but he knows that his talent for friendship, and his unfailing concern, are what he was engaged for, and that this is the thing the majority of the clients most need.

Naturally, the befriending of people who may be very disturbed is itself a skill which needs to be learned, but it can only be learned by those who already possess the human qualities which make them Samaritans. How friendship is most suitably manifested in a particular situation is something which comes from instruction and discussion, and from experience. It is not enough to be kindly and well-meaning, but just as those who have a good ear and a love of music can usually be taught to play different instruments, so the Samaritan type of person has a natural understanding and appreciation of the things which are explained in the Preparation Classes and Continuation Classes such as Case Conferences, and learns constantly both from his own experience and from observation of his colleagues in their dealings with clients. It does not usually happen that Samaritan types with few educational or intellectual advantages find themselves baffled by the psychology and other high-falutin' subjects which are discussed: the subjects do not appear to be difficult if they are presented in a Samaritan context to the volunteer who has a feeling for human relationships. Even the most unexpected revelations of the peculiar ways in which the mind can work are of fascinating interest to those who want to do their best for other human beings in abnormal mental or emotional states and are grasped almost intuitively. The instruction may not be remembered well enough for the person to reproduce it, but it will modify his practice and become a part of his manner of dealing with clients with the same lack of conscious application that one shows in riding a bicycle once one had got the knack. Just as a bright boy with an interest in mathematics will find the first steps in calculus fascinating and easy, so the natural Samaritan finds no difficulty in learning, for instance, that clients suffering from paranoid delusions of persecution must not be argued with, because any attempt to deal with their irrational beliefs by rational argument merely forces them to use all their usually considerable ingenuity in defending their delusional system, which is thereby deepened and extended. A Samaritan may or may not remember this but his natural sympathy with the client's distress will express itself in ways which quite unconsciously are impeccable from a psychological point of view, and over a period of befriending such a client the Samaritan may well be found to have built up and increased the sane areas of the client's thinking and his or her healthy interests. Indeed, there are some Samaritans who seem to know without being told how to deal with any kind of person whatever, for their natural gentleness, consideration, good manners and graciousness lead them safely past many pitfalls into which others of us might fall. But most Samaritans owe a great deal to the instruction they receive, and would be the first to admit that even sanctified commonsense is not always enough.

Applicants who get through the 'vetting interview' attend at least six Preparation Classes. These continue the organisation's selection procedure. All the Preparation Classes are about befriending: what it is, how it differs from counselling, what effects it has in particular cases, how it is best expressed in relation to particular psychological, sexual or other problems, how it fits in with and assists whatever counselling may also be undertaken for a client, how it can help clients to accept medical treatment when necessary or to benefit from any they may be receiving, what types of person cannot benefit from befriending at all, and what types can benefit so little that they are not really 'up The Samaritans' street'. During the Preparation Classes, the new volunteer not only learns a great deal that will be useful in the work but is also very likely to manifest any attitudes which would make him or her unsuitable for acceptance. This applies especially in Sensitivity Testing, in which groups of ten or a dozen gather with the conductor round a loud speaker, listening as they take turns in pairs at two distant telephones linked to the speaker through an amplifier. One plays the role of a client, and one of a Samaritan. This test is excellent for distinguishing those who can comfort a distressed person from those who can only deal cerebrally with the problem the person presents.

When applicants emerge from the Preparation Classes, they go on 'Observation Duty'. They think this is to permit them to observe what goes on, and of course it does, but it also allows them to be observed by experienced Samaritans. The new volunteers start in the probationary category of Helpers, because at this stage the organisation is not quite sure what they have in them and how close they are able to come to the Samaritan pattern.

The greatest amount is learned in practice. At Branch Meetings and in Continuation Classes volunteers are able to go much more deeply into the question of how to befriend, because problems which were academic in the Preparation Classes have now actually been encountered by the volunteers

B

in the course of their duties. The most important lessons of all, however, are learned by close association with those who are most truly Samaritans, and whose attitudes communicate themselves to those of the newer volunteers who are prepared to be influenced by their example, and show up those who aren't. 'How to be a Samaritan' is no longer something that was laid down by the founder of the organisation, but has become something which has been displayed in living actuality by a succession of dedicated volunteers whose communal personality is now 'The Samaritans'.

As soon as it appears reasonably likely that the Helpers have Samaritan qualities, and are also still keen, they are promoted to be Members.

Companions

In the London Branch and some others a few Members may be chosen to be admitted to 'The Company of Samaritans'. These are people who are judged to be natural Samaritans who can be depended upon to act as Samaritans in all circumstances and at all times. In each Branch, the first ones (there were six in the original London Branch) have to be chosen by the person in charge of the Branch, because there is no one else to do it, and these form the nucleus around which 'The Company of Samaritans' grows. Once formed, the 'Company' (not to be confused with the Limited Company which the whole Association technically is, though it is not called so) adds to its numbers by unanimous election by its existing members. The highest standards are demanded by the Company before any volunteer is elected to membership of it. Although election does not depend on the amount of activity, and has nothing whatever to do with seniority, most Companions manage to give more than the average amount of time to the organisation; but the chief consideration is always whether in the judgment of the Company the candidate *is* undoubtedly a Samaritan. One who is elected a Companion will have been judged to be loving and wise, charitable rather than sentimental, neither hard nor soft, utterly discreet and loyal, sufficiently humble to be surprised at being elected, but accepting the decision realistically and without question, sufficiently conscientious to 'reclassify' himself or herself in case of any failure to maintain the standard or because changed circumstances interfere with the work, and so devoted to the Company that if all the rest were to be travelling on a chartered plane that crashed, the one remaining would build it up again from the beginning.

People of this calibre are few and far between, but they do exist, and they exist in all walks of life and come from all kinds of backgrounds. They are found in all branches of the Christian Church and amongst adherents of the non-Christian faiths and amongst agnostics and humanists. They have more in common with one another than they have with other members of their own group who are not Samaritans.

It may rightly be supposed that the fellowship they develop amongst themselves is of a rare and precious quality, and that they become even more truly Samaritans by their association with one another. At their meetings, which no one else is permitted to attend except the person in charge of their Branch, who presides, they never take a vote: it would be unthinkable for a majority to impose its will on the minority. They continue their discussion, 'speaking the truth in love', until they arrive at a common mind, which the person in charge has the duty of expressing. If even one member finds himself or herself unable to agree, no decision is made. In particular no one is added to the Company if one of its existing members is even a little doubtful whether the person proposed is truly a Samaritan. It is realised that any Member who was disappointed or lost interest at not being elected a Companion would not deserve to be a Member at all, for every opportunity of serving the clients which a Companion enjoys is already available to him.

It is entirely in the spirit of the organisation that power-seekers are severely discouraged and authority exercised by those who desire it least. Naturally the Companions are given all the most difficult tasks and are as a matter of course treated with the least consideration. In the London Branch, where there may at times be a dozen volunteers on duty, the Samaritan-in-Charge will not necessarily be a Companion even if there are Companions on that duty. The talents which make a good Samaritan-in-Charge are possessed by some but not all Companions, and some but not all Members.

The effective working of a Branch depends upon the Branch Committee. If it has a Company of Samaritans, Companions are likely to be elected, which ensures that this Committee consists of people who are most concerned with the welfare of the clients and who are most determined that the soul of the movement should be embodied in the best examples of Samaritans that can be found.

Some people, of course, do not like the idea of the Company, saying that it is invidious to differentiate among the volunteers. 'Invidious' means 'tending to provoke envy, hatred, malice and all uncharitableness'. Any who can be provoked to these un-Samaritan attitudes should be identified and eliminated as soon as possible. We are not one of those worldly organisations which have to take account of seniority, efficiency, hurt pride and other false gods.

In the work of The Samaritans, it is essential to 'differentiate', and the only question is whether this should be done publicly or privately. There are some people who can be entrusted with any client, however difficult; others who are beginners, just feeling their feet; and others who can manage moderately difficult relationships with clients reasonably well. The person responsible for deploying the members to the best possible advantage of the client *must* have at least three categories in his mind, and the advantage of having them not in a secret book, but in a published list issued to all volunteers is that it is clear to all concerned who should be approached in particular circumstances and what kind of person the organisation is really looking for. Where a Company of Samaritans exists its life and spirit are the life and spirit of the whole organisation. There is no way of getting into it except by unanimous election by the existing members. Admission cannot be gained by money or influence or wire-pulling, and not even by frantic activity in the work of the organisation. Volunteers in the organisation go quietly on with their work without worrying about 'promotion', and those who cannot help being in the fullest sense Samaritans may be recognised as such, and be elected to the Company; otherwise they will continue to work equally devotedly in the category of Member. Not the least of the advantages of this arrangement is that aggressive, self-important, committee-minded or power-seeking individuals, who are not wanted in the organisation anyway, quickly realise that it is an organisation in which they will not get very far.

The Council of Management resolved in 1965 (a) that all members should be called 'Samaritans'; (b) that in all Branches the volunteers should serve for a probationary period as *Samaritan Helpers* before being classified as *Samaritan Members*; (c) that those Branches which choose to do so may have a third category of volunteers called *Samaritan Companions*, members of a Company of Samaritans which elects its own members; (d) that the classification *Samaritan Leaders* should include not only Directors and Deputy Directors, but also lay Leaders who may make the third category of volunteers unnecessary in Branches with a number of such Leaders; and (e) that the classification *Samaritan Consultant* should be used for persons attached to the Branch in an advisory capacity. Volunteers engage in befriending and interviewing: they are not employed in counselling, unless, in exceptional cases, they have qualifications for this. Counselling is done by selected Leaders and Consultants; but the chief function of the Leaders is to select, instruct, and supervise the volunteers, making sure that these are not left with the burden of making decisions that they are not competent to make, and do not become anxious about those entrusted to them to befriend.

The whole atmosphere of The Samaritans is *sui generis*. Most of the standards of the world are rejected. Just as in an internment camp – another instance of people being up against the harsh realities of life and death together – nothing is important except the humanity of each person, for those who have money cannot get at it, those who have fine clothes at home are in the same rags as everyone else, all eat the same food and either share or do not share with the weak and the sick, so in The Samaritans nobody is interested in your money or title or accent or the importance of your job, but only in whether you are a person whom merely to be with will make the clients feel hopeful again.

Your religion (or lack of it), your political affiliations and other irrelevant matters will not be mentioned to the clients, and your colleagues are unlikely to discover about these, except by chance, because you will have more important things to talk about with them. Somewhere buried in the files is your application form, on which your religion, if any, is mentioned, only because it might happen that a client wished to speak with someone of the same faith as himself. In that case, someone would have to look it up. Proselytising is strictly forbidden: hardly ever does a client want to be evangelised, and although all human beings have needs that may be described as 'spiritual', these are not met by trotting out ready-made answers to questions that have not been asked.

The Samaritans is not a church organisation, nor a Christian organisation: it comprises amongst its membership people of all faiths and of no explicit faith, and whilst in a nominally Christian country a slight majority are Christians of one sort or another, this is not true of its membership in other countries. The fact that its name and its inspiration come from a parable in the Christian Gospel is of less significance than the fact that that particular parable appeals deeply to all men and women of goodwill everywhere, no matter what religion they may profess or fail to profess.

In England, a decreasing number of Branches have their headquarters in Church premises. Because it is essential that they should be situated in the centre of large cities where office accommodation is expensive, the crypt or vestry or hall of a church was often chosen as the most economical form of office accommodation in the most expensive part of a big town. Now that the value of the work the Samaritans do is officially recognised, secular premises are common, sometimes in the shape of a house provided by the local authority. One or two Branches own purpose-built premises, and the London Branch has the Crypt of St Stephen Walbrook leased to it for 99 years.

The vast majority of Samaritan Directors used to be

clergymen, because of all the professions other than the medical profession, which can only be used in a consultative capacity in a non-medical organisation, the profession 'Minister of Religion' was the one which lent itself best to the type of work a Director has to do. This is not to say that more than a small minority of clergymen and ministers are suitable for running a Samaritan Branch: many are too rigid or too ecclesiastical, or feel themselves to be called to a definitely evangelistic or exclusively pastoral ministry. It is noteworthy that those clergy and ministers who *do* feel called to serve as Samaritan Directors, and are found suitable for the work, are very much of one mind, irrespective of the denomination from which they come. They are notably un-parsonical, and most of them do not wear clerical collars in the centre, for fear of frightening off some sensitive client. At the time of writing, the number of non-clerical Directors has almost caught up with the number of clerical ones, and a third of the former are women.

The fellowship, transcending denominational and other barriers, which exists among the volunteers is also found at Directors' Conferences and at Schools for Leaders. These now include a proportion of non-Christian Directors and Deputy Directors, united in a fellowship of service in which the members, each loyal to his or her own convictions and community, work together in harmony and mutual respect, learning humbly from one another and never seeking to score points off one another or pretending to have a mono-poly of truth. Whilst those in authority in the various religious bodies rightly seek formally for reunion, ordinary people from the rank and file are already enjoying the kind of fellowship without which any reunion would be a mere outward form.

Setting up a Branch

The way in which a new Branch is set up is now prescribed by the Council of Management of The Samaritans (Inc.) on the basis of years of experience in different places, and a brochure issued. The initiative has in the past come either from a doctor or clergyman or other influential person, or from a body such as a Clergy and Ministers' Fraternal, Council of Christian Congregations, or in one or two cases from a Borough Health Committee. Where an enthusiastic enquirer is not in a position of influence, he is invited to try to interest someone who is. In due course a Steering Committee is formed, which arranges either an Invitation Meeting to which the sort of people who might become Leaders or Consultants are invited, or a Public Meeting which anyone, as well as these, may attend; or both. Once the decision is made to try to establish a Branch in the area, and a Committee, with a Convenor, is elected, the Council of Management may recognise this Committee and those associated with it as a Preparatory Group. This Group is entitled to use the name of The Samaritans in its publicity, and it has the task of finding an Acting Director (who must be approved by the Association) and other Leaders, Consultants (this is the easiest task) and, above all, volunteers, for whom a course of Preparation Classes is arranged by the Association. The Committee meanwhile seeks suitable premises, obtains an easily memorised telephone number, and raises the necessary funds.

As soon as all this has been done and a sufficient number of volunteers selected and instructed, a date is fixed for the service to come into operation by the emergency number being advertised, and the Preparatory Group, with the approval of the Association, becomes a Probationary Branch as from this date. Branches remain probationary, with non-voting observers instead of voting representatives on the Council of Management of the Association, for at least a year, and the Director remains an Acting Director until he has attended one of the schools for Directors, or one of the annual Conferences, or some equivalent occasion which allows the Association to satisfy itself that he knows his job and is himself a 'Samaritan type'.

The Executive Committee of the Council of Management arranges for every branch to be visited annually by two of a panel of Visitors, to maintain communication between the branches and the Executive and to encourage the Members in their work, as well as to ensure that the principles and methods of the Association are working well in that Branch. The Council of Management interferes as little as possible with the branches, because in emergency work the people on the spot must make their own decisions. It tries only to ensure that centres using the Samaritan name should be recognisably the same everywhere, inspired by the same spirit, and differing only as local circumstances require; and it preserves the Samaritan ethos not by detailed regulations and directives, but by retaining the appointment of the Director (or Chairman) of each Branch in its own hands, on the recommendation of the Branch Committee. Directors are appointed or re-appointed each year, and this is not automatic: the Association has a plain duty to appoint the person who will help the clients most by making the Branch as truly 'Samaritan' as it can be.

Client-centred structure of The Samaritans

The whole organisation is client-centred. The clients are its sole *raison d'être*: it has no other object, main or subsidiary, than to serve the clients in such a way that they will stay alive and be glad to be alive and be enabled to live 'more abundantly'. Every detail of the methods and principles of The Samaritans has been worked out in the light of clients' actual needs as discovered by experience, and instructions about ways of working are normally conveyed to those concerned in the words: 'The needs of the clients dictate that . . .'. The Director of a Branch may appear to be a dictator, and his authority is unquestioned in a Samaritan Branch, because the needs of the clients dictate that decisions should be swiftly made and loyally executed without dithering, for 'in the multitude of counsellors there is confusion'. But standing over every Director is his dictator, an amalgamation of the clients with whom he has had to deal and from whom he has learnt by patient and imaginative observation what clients need.

Clients contemplating suicide need to be able to get in touch at any time with a minimum of effort: hence the emergency telephone. They need to be able to 'test the temperature' before committing themselves: hence the possibility of remaining anonymous at the beginning of the conversation, or indefinitely, if they wish. They need to retain their freedom of action and to remain in control of their own destinies whilst still having some sort of help: hence the confidentiality, and the assurance that nothing whatever will be done against their will – no one will pick them up in a plain van and lock them up in a padded cell, or even call and see them without their permission. They need a friend to turn to, who will simply be that and nothing more unless and until they express a wish for something more from someone in the organisation: hence the provision that the telephone is answered in the first instance by a volunteer – not a doctor, for they may have rung because they do not want to ring a doctor, and not a parson or social worker, for the same reason. They need someone who can get them more expert help if this is required: hence the structure of the organisation, and the other, non-emergency telephone with another member to use it. They may need someone to go to them who cannot leave the telephone: hence the 'Flying Squad' (see p. 52). They may need to speak to someone of a different sex or age or kind from the one who first answered: hence the mixture of volunteers on duty. They may need to talk to someone more expert at once, perhaps in the middle of the night: hence 'Home Service'. They may need to ring several times till they hear a voice that inspires confidence: hence the duty roster with its constant changes, and the refusal to log heavy breathing or incoherent sobs as a hoax. They need above all to know that they have nothing to lose, and perhaps everything to gain, by ringing The Samaritans: hence the care with which the volunteers are chosen, deployed, instructed and supervised.

In a word, they need love.

Different approaches to suicide prevention

How love is to express itself is a matter on which not all who 'feel a concern' for the potentially suicidal are agreed. There are some who are convinced that only medically qualified people ought to encounter the potential suicide in an emergency situation, because of the high proportion of cases of mental illness and the inability of unqualified people to make diagnoses. The Samaritans can only welcome the establishment of medical emergency centres for the suicidal, for the people who approach these are by hypothesis willing to recognise their need of a doctor; but they do not believe that such a centre can make The Samaritans unnecessary, for it is a fact of experience that many suicidal persons will not entertain the idea of psychiatry, and also that some who may accept psychiatry have other needs which a doctor cannot supply but which The Samaritans sometimes can.

At the other extreme, there are those who are convinced that the potential suicide who seeks non-medical help is to be regarded as a person with a spiritual problem, whether he recognises this or not, and that the object of emergency aid by telephone should be to lead him to acceptance of the Christian Faith in the form in which this is held by the Church or group of Churches responsible for the service.

The Samaritans have many objections to this. First, it does not get to grips with the problem of suicide, for it is just not true that any large proportion of potential suicides can be deterred by evangelisation, and if some suicidal people are helped, it will be because of the attention they receive from persons who in many cases are kindly as well as pious, rather than because of the preaching of the Gospel in words. Secondly, it leaves out of account not only those who may need psychiatric help but also members of non-Christian faiths, members of Churches with which the Church or group of Churches offering the service have little in com-mon, and the even larger category of those who, though nominally Christians, distrust the Church for the very reason that they suspect that its representatives *will* seek to serve its own interests rather than serve the client disinterestedly. Thirdly, it leads to the scandal of rival services, e.g. Roman Catholic and Protestant, in the same city. Fourthly, it tends to become clerical: in the Swedish 'Jourhavende Pastor' (which means 'Priest on duty'), it is not surprising that priests answer the telephone. Fifthly, though it may attract some volunteers who have a 'Samaritan' spirit, it must attract others whose main objective is the making of converts.

45

Sixthly, some of those whose offer to help could hardly be declined by such a service, because of their impeccable religious qualifications, would be rejected by The Samaritans on the ground that their approach would tend to make some clients feel even more guilty and more unworthy, and thus increase the risk of suicide.

Naturally, any group of people has the right to organise a centre which the general public is invited to telephone, for any purpose the law allows. Such a group can direct its invitation specially to the suicidal if it wishes, provided it does not use the name 'The Samaritans' or 'The Telephone Samaritans', which are registered by our Association. (The many other societies which incorporate the word 'Samaritan' are not concerned with the prevention of suicide by emergency telephone.)

Relations with the Press

The vast majority of those who apply to The Samaritans for help are fortunately people whose situation The Samaritans are able to ameliorate, and for a not inconsiderable number Samaritan help has made all the difference between living and dying. The proportion of clients applying to a particular Samaritan Branch depends to a great extent on the amount of publicity which has been received by the Branch at that period.

Those Branches which use posters or paid advertisements have, of course, control over the material, and in the case of radio and television programmes, which are usually pre-recorded, it is possible to ensure roughly the kind of presentation the organisation desires. In the case of Press or magazine publicity, interviews are freely granted to reporters and agencies, and there is often no control over the use made of the material supplied. Thus, however carefully the interviewee may have expressed himself, a somewhat misleading impression may be given, either by the emphasis on what seems more sensational and the suppression of the rest, or by cuts made in an otherwise balanced story. There seems to be no way of avoiding this, and the movement has been most fortunate in having almost invariably the goodwill and co-operation of journalists.

If, however, a Press report fails to make it clear that the whole service is confidential and that the client remains in charge of his or her own destiny, some clients will be deterred from making an approach; and if the kind of help The Samaritans do *not* offer, such as financial help, is mentioned, the number of clients asking for money or writing begging letters is enormously increased. The fault is by no means always with reporters and sub-editors when this kind of thing has happened: it requires a certain amount of experience to *be* interviewed successfully by the Press, and beginners have sometimes said things they did not mean or failed to make themselves clear.

It is in order to avoid this kind of difficulty that Press enquiries are always referred to the leadership, and volunteers are not allowed to give interviews unless these are arranged by the Director. The movement owes a great debt of gratitude to the Press for keeping the work of The Samaritans fairly regularly before the public, even though the nature of the work makes it impossible to give to the Press those 'case histories' which would make a story really interesting from their point of view, but which might deter clients from coming because of the fear that some such 'case history', unless in the most general terms, might be recognised by their friends and applied to themselves.

Reporters generally know their job, and the best of them

have written stories far better than any we could have written for ourselves. If sometimes we have been a little squeamish about the way things were put, that did not really matter as long as the story was effective in bringing in clients. For instance, in about 1954 a well-written article in a London evening paper was given a headline (not by the writer of it) which I thought a bit vulgar. It appeared over a photograph of me, and ran, 'The parson who can't be shocked.' I felt very differently about it when large numbers of clients came along, most of them saying, 'I have come to you because they say you can't be shocked.' Ten or more years later a headline in a Belfast paper said of the volunteers, 'They listen while people talk themselves out of trouble.' We could not have put it better.

It is sometimes said that 'there is no such thing as bad publicity' – that as long as people are talking about an organisation or a product, it will help to make the organisation known or sell the product, even if what is said is disparaging or inaccurate. I think this cannot apply to a voluntary service which has to attract nervous people. It would do the movement a great deal of harm if a newspaper report gave the impression that, although The Samaritans offer strict confidentiality to clients, if someone confessed to a crime the Samaritans' duty as citizens would take precedence over their undertaking to the organisation, so that criminals would be handed over to the police. People who have committed crimes of various kinds *are* amongst the clients of The Samaritans, and although they may be led to discuss the pros and cons of giving themselves up and facing the music with a Samaritan by their side, they will in no circumstances be handed over or any information given about them without their consent. The volunteer conveys all confessions of crime (which may be true or false, and being hearsay, are not evidence) to the Director and then forgets all about them. The Director is accustomed to such situations, and is not likely to be stampeded into any rash statement. He (or she) also knows that it might happen that refusal to testify might lead to imprisonment for contempt.

Relations with the medical profession

The Samaritans enjoy very good relations with the medical profession, largely because doctors know that they make no attempt to trespass on medical fields, and that they encourage clients to have confidence in the treatment prescribed by their own doctor. On the rare occasions when the client's own doctor does not appear to be interested or to take seriously the client's desire for psychiatric attention, a way round is found without any criticism being made or implied about the doctor concerned. If a client changes his doctor, this is his own idea, not something suggested by The Samaritans. Every effort is made to persuade clients who seem to require psychiatry to allow their own doctor to arrange it, and only if they flatly refuse to permit their doctor to be approached (or if they do not have one in the same town) is a direct appointment sought for them. In the very large cities, there are more of such cases than in smaller towns, and also easier access to psychiatry via Casualty or Out-Patient Clinics. The vast majority of doctors are more concerned with the welfare of human beings than with the letter of their rights, and we have hardly ever had complaints arising out of the rare situations where a doctor did not know that a patient had seen a psychiatirst until the psychiatrist (who may not be bound by the client's wishes as we are) notified him of this.

The Samaritans not only enjoy the co-operation of many

doctors and the tolerance of most, but increasingly have patients recommended to them by both general practitioners and psychiatrists for the befriending which the doctor knows they urgently need. An American psychiatrist has stated that when prescribing for a patient he often wished to include TLC, which is not in the pharmacopoeia, but stands for 'tender loving care'. Most of us have this from our families and friends, but for those who possess neither, it is difficult to come by. This is why so large a proportion of our mental hospital beds are occupied by patients who no longer need any treatment but who, if discharged, would soon be driven back by the same circumstances that brought them there in the first place.

Every Samaritan Branch has at least one Medical Consultant, usually a psychiatrist, to advise the Directors, Deputy Directors or other Leaders, and in some cases actually to see clients whose problem appears to be a medical one.

Psychological problems fall into three main groups: psychotic, psychoneurotic and psychopathic. No one seems to know what to do about the grossly psychopathic except to protect society from them, but most of the psychoses and neuroses have an appropriate form of treatment, whether by physical means or by psychotherapy, or a combination of both. People suffering from a psychotic illness seem not amenable to psychotherapy, but medical treatments are often effective. The main forms of these illnesses are the schizophrenias, the paranoid states, and the manic-depressive illnesses, including endogenous depression. All these need medical treatment, and nothing else will do. The Samaritans are often successful in persuading sufferers from these illnesses to undergo treatment, and the one which most frequently leads to suicide, namely depressive illness, is the one which fortunately seems to respond best. Samaritan befriending may be helpful in the case of many psychotic illnesses. The various neuroses, such as anxiety states and the various phobias, may be so severe as to require medical treatment, or may respond to psychotherapy or psychological counselling, by someone who may or may not be a doctor. As all of us are to some extent neurotic, in the sense that we make use of various defences and pretences and evasions in trying to cope with the world, the category 'normal', if used at all, must be defined as 'neurotic, but not to an incapacitating degree'. The neurotic person, unlike the psychotic, has not retreated into a world of delusion but is still living in the same world as most of us, though finding life difficult in various ways. Befriending has a very great part to play in helping those suffering from neuroses, especially the less severe ones which have to be lived with because it has been decided to 'let sleeping dogs lie'.

What happens when a client rings up?

Whether by day or by night, whether in a large or small branch, what is aimed at is that the person who answers the telephone when a client rings shall be a volunteer, i.e. a fellow human being who cares. Even in the London Branch, which has a small full-time staff during office hours, Monday to Friday, the emergency telephones are always answered by a volunteer. Some of the smaller branches have difficulty in finding sufficient volunteers to man the telephone during working hours, and are therefore compelled to use Leaders for this purpose, but generally speaking a client expects that when he telephones he will be answered by an ordinary Samaritan, not by a parson, doctor, social worker or other expert, and his expectation is seldom disappointed.

The volunteer who answers the telephone does not attempt

to obtain all the information about the client and his problem in detailed form in order to 'solve' the problem. He is content to listen, to be sympathetic, and to make the client feel that he is personally interested in the client's well-being and concerned about the client's unhappiness. Naturally, in most cases a good deal of information is given and is entered on a Report Form.

The main purpose of the first conversation on the telephone is to avert the immediate crisis, establish rapport and, if it seems the right thing, win the client's confidence sufficiently to persuade him or her to come and be seen face to face. Those clients who wish to remain anonymous voices on the telephone may do so, but only a minority make this decision, and some of those later change their mind and decide to trust The Samaritans with their identity and their address, knowing that no use will be made of this information without their permission. If the call is during the night, and the client cannot be invited to come to the office but it is essential that he see someone at once, a volunteer (not one who is tied to the telephone by being on Night Watch) will be sent to him. Whether the volunteer goes alone or with others this is described as 'Flying Squad', and the more dangerous the area covered (Soho, for example) the more likely it is that the 'Squad' will consist of one apparently frail but intrepid woman. Flying Squad may not be called out by Night Watch without permission from 'Home Service', which means the Samaritan-in-Charge that night on duty by his or her home telephone.

Sooner or later, in the office or elsewhere, the client almost always meets an experienced Member, and, in the course of an interview lasting about an hour, the facts of the situation will be ascertained in a befriending context and will be incorporated in a report on the standard form. The Samaritan-in-

Charge will check this report, and the person whose duty it is will read it fairly soon afterwards, and make a decision as to what is to be done to help the client, and who is to do it. If it is considered appropriate, someone will be allocated to befriend the client. If counselling is thought necessary, an appointment will be made for this (perhaps in addition to befriending), and if the client needs to see a doctor, and is willing to do so, arrangements for this will be made. In any event, a responsible person will be in charge of that particular client's case, and will arrange and supervise whatever befriending or other ministrations he is to have. If ongoing befriending has been authorised the volunteer doing the befriending keeps in regular touch with the person in charge of the case and works under his or her direction.

The purpose of befriending is not to remain in this relationship for the rest of the client's life. It could be said that the purpose of befriending is to make itself unnecessary, by bringing out those potentialities for good human relationships in the client which at the time he first came were not in evidence. Befriending continues as long as the person in charge considers that it will be beneficial to the client, and, if it is successfuly done, sooner or later the client will be able to make his or her own friends and the Samaritan befriender can be withdrawn and allocated to someone else.

The Samaritans exist to deal with the acute crises in people's lives, not in order to give lifetime support to the chronically inadequate. This is not because the chronically inadequate do not need befriending, but because the kind of befriending from which they can benefit is different from the kind offered by the Samaritans, who are geared to deal with emergencies and think in terms of contact with a client for weeks and months rather than years. The befriending of the chronically inadequate, which may produce 1 per cent improvement per annum in some cases, needs to be done by a reasonably near neighbour, and it ought not to be too much to expect Christian and other congregations to take responsibility for the chronically inadequate in their neighbourhood. Their befriending will often involve frequent contact with welfare services and can be done under the guidance of trained people. At present, many who fall into this category take up a great deal of additional time with welfare workers because they look to *them* for the befriending which they are not receiving in their own neighbourhood.

An organisation dedicated to the prevention of suicide must not dissipate its energies by widening its terms of reference to such an extent as to impair the service it is offering in its chosen field. The entire human resources of many branches could be used up by a hundred inadequate personalities bordering on the psychopathic, only a handful of whom would ever get near to being suicide risks. Just as in a railway accident rescue workers would concentrate on those who were severely injured and possibly bleeding to death, leaving people with sprains and bruises to less skilled people, so the Samaritans, who have been assembled in order to deal as much as possible with matters of life and death, dare not let themselves be bogged down with other matters which people who have not been mobilised for this urgent task can deal with equally well.

If they are to fulfil their purpose, Samaritans must not be sentimental, but realistic. They would be failing in their duty if they were to adopt some such slogan as 'No one is ever turned away'. If aggressive male and hysteric female psychopaths were not turned away, no one else would ever get any attention. If purely welfare cases were not referred to the appropriate organisation which exists to help them, The Samaritans would become an amateur and inefficient casework agency and thus fail to make their own unique contribution. If Samaritans attempted to do badly what specialist organisations do well, instead of enjoying the goodwill and co-operation of these, they would be regarded by them with justifiable suspicion.

However, the client's wishes must be granted where possible, even if he or she insists on having, for example, marital counselling from members of The Samaritans, refusing to be referred to a Marriage Guidance Council – not that this body would claim any monopoly of marriage guidance, which has long been performed by the clergy and others. It remains desirable in principle that The Samaritans should be seen not as a rival to any existing service but as providing a service which but for them would not exist. One of the reasons for the rapid spread and growth of the movement is that there was a desperate need which was not being met.

Naturally, it is not possible for the Samaritans to confine their activities exclusively to those who are in imminent danger of taking their own life. Just as a considerable number of applicants to join the organisation has to be 'processed' in order to discover first the possibles, then the probables, then the ones who are to the best of our judgment certainties, so a considerable number of callers have to be dealt with in order to ensure that amongst them there are some who might, and some who would, have killed themselves if The Samaritans had not been there to help them.

That is why our letter heading says 'The Samaritans – to befriend the suicidal and despairing'. No one who is feeling desperate need hesitate to get in touch with The Samaritans because he cannot lay his hand on his heart and swear an affidavit that he is on the point of killing himself. It is sufficient for The Samaritans that he is very distressed: he does not need to threaten or attempt suicide in order to persuade them to take his situation to heart. But there is all the difference in the world between those who are in such a state that it would not be surprising if they were weary of life and whose situation can be transformed by the ministrations of The Samaritans, and those who are unfortunately unable to benefit from the kind of help the Samaritans offer and go round in many cases from one agency to another not seriously wanting or being capable of any real improvement.

The proportion of 'serious suicide risks' varies in different branches of The Samaritans between 5 and 35 per cent of the clients: the average being about 10 per cent. Something like 20 per cent are in a situation where they might commit suicide sooner or later unless something is done now; and there are also some who are very unhappy indeed but who, for conscientious reasons, would never make a suicidal act. In addition, there is a varying proportion of more or less 'inadequate' people who come to The Samaritans in times of crisis which recur at intervals, and who seem to benefit to some extent from periodical attention. No Branch, however, can perform its task effectively if it allows the time and energies of its members to be taken up interminably by people who have come to 'the wrong shop', and the army of chronic scroungers and unrepentant confidence tricksters is as much out of place in a Samaritan centre as would be a ward full of patients suffering from senile dementia – not because there is nothing that these people need, but because what they need is something the Samaritans are not organised and do not exist to supply.

Unless it is clear from the outset that a person is grossly psychopathic, or has obviously misunderstood the nature of the organisation, a decision whether The Samaritans can help or not is made only when the situation has become clear. When a client has to be told that there is nothing, or nothing further, that The Samaritans can usefully do, it may be that some small service is performed by volunteers bearing the resentment and abuse which are sometimes vented on them, and which are a very understandable expression of a person's frustration, especially if he is immature, or implacably unwilling to co-operate in his own interests.

The sympathetic ear

Many clients are emotionally disturbed rather than mentally ill. They are not suffering primarily from some diagnosable and treatable mental condition, but are upset or agitated or depressed or confused because of some untoward circumstance or set of circumstances which they can no longer cope with alone. In these cases, though counselling may be of value, the most important thing is Samaritan befriending of the highest quality available. It is a great comfort in times of emotional distress to have a sympathetic person who will simply be with you and metaphorically hold your hand and refrain from giving you advice or telling you to pull yourself together when your problem is that you cannot pull yourself together. In some cases it is possible to give practical help in modifying the circumstances which have caused the distress, for instance by being instrumental in effecting a reconciliation between two people who have quarrelled, or suffered from some misunderstanding; or in sorting out problems relating to the person's work. Without attempting to engage amateurishly in casework, the volunteer can often, either directly or through the leadership, arrange for some at least of the client's worries to be removed or lessened.

Sexual problems (including marital problems, which nearly always have a sexual basis) account for 3 out of every

8 of the more serious cases, and are only outnumbered by the psychological problems, many of them of course with some sexual content, which account for 4 out of 8 – though only 1 of these 4 is psychiatric, i.e. requiring medical treatment as distinct from psychotherapy or psychological counselling. Of the sexual problems other than marital, the commonest is homosexuality, which of itself causes great distress in many cases, though it is a less desperate condition than it was before our laws were made more enlightened in respect of males. Amongst young people, there are worries about masturbation, unwanted pregnancy and fear of V.D., and amongst the middle-aged there are problems of impotence, alleged frigidity, and all kinds of frustration. People with sexual problems tend to feel excessively guilty, and often regard themselves as being beyond the pale, so that they require particularly gentle handling. The attitude of acceptance which Samaritan volunteers are taught to show to all clients is particularly important in the case of those with sexual problems, which clients may be ashamed to speak of at all unless the person they encounter inspires confidence, and is neither pruriently curious nor condemnatory.

Particularly in the larger cities, Samaritans have to be prepared to listen sympathetically and without being shocked to clients suffering from every deviation of aim or object in the textbooks, of some of which the volunteer may barely have heard. Fetishism, sado-masochism, voyeurism, exhibitionism, rape suffered or committed, incest, animality, transvestism, change of sex, male and female prostitution, are all things which may lead a human being into a state where he or she just has to talk to someone who will not turn away in horror or stupidly suppose that the client must be having a wonderful time. All these things appear very different to one who is faced by a worried, shame-ridden fellow human being, from what they seem when hinted at or gloated over or (as a painful duty) 'exposed' with simulated horror in the more sensational Sunday newspapers. People who like 'normal' sex are the fortunate ones rather than the virtuous ones.

Nobody should join The Samaritans who is going to be put off by four-letter words or other forms of verbal aggressiveness or ribaldry. It is understandable if unprotected young girls, plagued by obscene telephone calls to their flats, appeal to the police to try to catch the person, but it is entirely different when such calls are made to The Samaritans. Women living alone or without a man about the house are liable to think that the caller is a huge caveman who will follow up his call by coming round and raping them, but volunteers in The Samaritans have no excuse for panicking, since they have learnt in the preparation classes that such characters are nearly always frightened little chaps who dare not even say, 'Nice weather we've been having' to a girl if they met one face to face. These are pitiable people, who need help, and a Samaritan volunteer tries to persuade them of this, and convince them that they will not be walking into any trap if they come round to discuss their sexual difficulties with us. What appears in one's own home to be a horrid intrusion takes on a very different complexion when one is on duty in the office of an organisation which exists to help people in every kind of difficulty arising out of poor human relationships. Those men who *do*, after receiving the same sort of answer from several different people, pluck up courage to come round and talk about their problem, are usually so easy to help that it is a pity so many of them just cannot believe that the whole thing is not a trick to get them arrested or beaten up.

One of the most difficult things for most of us to learn is how to bear the griefs and distresses of others, and to go on bearing these with them and for them until the whole load has been unburdened. The temptation is to intervene every time the client pauses for breath or to collect his thoughts, with some words of 'reassurance'. I have put the word in inverted commas because it is not the client who is being reassured, but the person who ought to be sharing his burdens and instead is throwing each one back, finding it too heavy and pretending that it is not as heavy as is being suggested. 'Count your blessings, it's not as bad as you think' merely adds insult to injury. You insult a fellow human being by telling him that the things which have brought him almost to the verge of suicide are not as bad as all that.

A real Samaritan is prepared to listen, and go on listening, and refrain from interrupting, and keep his bright suggestions until the end, when they will probably be seen to be un-necessary or irrelevant anyway, and be willing to bear and share the pain of it all with the sufferer without complaining that it is too much. Quite often, the mere fact of having been heard out, of somebody having listened and gone on listening until the whole story has been told, of being with somebody who cared enough to let it all become part of himself or herself, is all that is needed. The client goes away without having received any advice whatever but with more faith and hope and courage than he had when he came.

This is the purest kind of Samaritan work, bearing and forbearing and sympathising in the literal sense of 'suffering with' a fellow human being. The client thought nobody cared, or at least that nobody cared enough, but he has found someone who does care, enough to make the attempt to go on living worth while. The theme song of many such clients could be, in the words of *Songs of Couch and Consulta-*

tion, 'It's not that I haven't been loved, I haven't been loved *enough* to make me feel most properly loved.'

Directive and non-directive therapy

I am convinced that the best therapy is non-directive, but I shall not be doctrinaire about it, for I find there are times when it is kindest to use whatever authority you have, particularly in situations where a person is just incapable of making a decision for himself and when a decision must be made. It is like teaching a child to walk: if you do not let it go for fear it will fall and hurt itself, it will never learn, but it you go to the other extreme, it might fall into the fire. It is not only children who *need* at times to be told what to do, but also adults whom circumstances have brought almost to the helpless dependence of childhood, though of course this dependence must be ended as rapidly as possible. It seems to me that if you have some authority, you are bound to influence those who consult you, whether you use it to direct bewildered or frightened people what step to take next, or whether, as more often happens, you use it 'non-directively', i.e. to direct the person to consider with you what step he wants to take. Mostly it is better to let the other person take as long as he needs to find out what it is that *he* wants to do.

I remember one woman who was so verbose that no one ever listened to her. When she came to see me, she was talking before the door opened, and did not stop for well over an hour. She did not even pause to take a drink of the tea I offered her, lest I should slip a word in edgeways. At first this torrent of words was incoherent and repetitious, but gradually, as I continued to give her my full attention, the nature of her quite complicated situation began to be clarified. She was by no means unintelligent, but like some people doing an addition sum, she could only think if she did it aloud. At long last she paused, and took a drink of her cold tea. All the time she had been talking I had been sorting out her problems, and I was quite pleased with the cleverness of my solution. Now was my big chance, and I took it: I said nothing. She put down her cup, stood up and shook me warmly by the hand, and told me mine was the best advice she had ever had and she would go away and do exactly as I had suggested and was sure it would work out splendidly.

Throughout the interview I had not said a word, unless you count 'Mmmm'. That does not mean I had not said anything: my attention to her conveyed sympathy with her plight and respect for her good intentions. Most people who ask for advice do not want advice, they want approval for what they are going to do anyway; and this I gave her. I do not suppose anyone had ever bothered to hear her out before.

I might have felt a pang for my own beautiful solution if I had not still been ashamed of an occasion a few weeks before when I had gone with a chap to a difficult encounter to speak on his behalf, and the other person had not allowed me to speak, so I had to listen whilst the client said badly what I flattered myself I would have said well. We got what we came for, and I did some soul searching and reminded myself that the object of our journey was this, and not to demonstrate what a good advocate I was. It is a blessing that duties come too thick and fast to allow time for the temptation to pat oneself on the back when one of them has been done successfully – or, for that matter, for profitless repining over failures.

An example of direction succeeding where non-directive methods would not have been quick enough, if they had worked at all, was in the case of a young woman who was not going to deserve that adjective much longer and whose first, and probably last, chance of marriage had come whilst her widowed mother, with whom she lived, still needed her. The mother was evidently one of those sweet tyrants who are more frustrating than sour ones: a sofa invalid whom I guessed to be as tough as old boots, living on her daughter's vitality and, like a vampire, getting younger as the latter got older. There was no financial or even servant problem, but the mother had convinced her daughter that to leave her in order to get married (which would involve moving some way away) would cause the mother's death. The conflict between her 'duty' to her mother and her desire for a life of her own with the man she loved had led her to a suicidal act which nearly proved fatal, and I was not slow to point out that if she had died, neither of them would have had her. The conflict could be resolved only by her seeing one claim as a duty and the other as an occasion of sin, and I told her firmly that she must let her suitor marry her and take her away, because it was bad for her mother's soul as well as her own that she should remain tied to someone she hated. 'But I love Mama!' she protested. 'Nonsense,' I said. 'Nobody could love that selfish old bloodsucker, and I bet your father's death was a blessed release for him. She's conditioned you to believe it's your duty to "love" her in the sense of pandering to all her whims, but if you didn't think it was wicked to say so you'd admit you hate her.' After a while she said quietly, 'Yes, I hate her', and I had a glimpse of her private hell from which the only escape was suicide, or murder – unless a man firmly carried her away. For once I became a Bible-thumper. 'Therefore,' I quoted, 'shall a man leave his father and mother, and cleave unto his wife!' 'But I'm not a man,' she objected unconvincingly. 'The point is,'

I asked, 'does he make you feel a woman?' The way she looked as she answered 'Yes' gave me hope that we had won, and so it proved. A year later the marriage was still happy and the mother still cumbering the earth. 'Tell my story,' the daughter said, 'if you think it might help someone else.' There are, of course, a lot of people who would do well to show *more* consideration for their parents, which is why probably nothing could have prised that young woman loose in time except a priest prophesying at her forcefully about God's will. I also gave her a briefing on sex in marriage, so she had a carrot in front as well as a goad behind.

One thing the experienced Samaritan volunteer will never do is to make light of something which is obviously causing the client great concern. People do often worry themselves sick about something which may appear to another person to be comparatively trivial, but if the volunteer regards it as trivial when told about it, it means that he is failing to put himself in the other person's place and look at things from his point of view. A Samaritan does not normally say such things as, 'If I were you, I would do so-and-so', but if it *should* be right to say this he would *mean*, 'If I were you', and not, 'If you were me'. The Samaritan in the parable went where the injured man was, and the Samaritan volunteer has to go where the client is and be with him there, and not beckon him over to come where the Samaritan is.

Spiritual help

In any Branch which is seriously getting to grips with its job, the proportion of spiritual problems will be low, because although many people have spiritual problems, these do not as frequently lead to suicide as do psychological and sexual problems and problems of loneliness. Churchgoers form only about 10 per cent of the population, and among the clients of The Samaritans the proportion is much less than this. It looks as though religious faith is, as one might expect, something which, where it exists, gives meaning and purpose to life and is therefore some protection against suicidal impulses; but it is not something which can be handed out like a dose of medicine.

Since the object of The Samaritans is the prevention of suicide, the organisation is primarily concerned with those problems which most predispose to suicide, and any conscious spiritual need is usually a very minor part of the troubles that bring people to The Samaritans. The religious members of the organisation do not preach religion to their clients. If a client firmly and explicitly *asks* for religious instruction, this is arranged, and the agnostic members would be as assiduous in arranging this as a teetotal member would be in standing a client a drink (unless the client was an alcoholic in the latter case or a religious maniac in the former).

Leaning over backwards to avoid inflicting personal beliefs on the client sometimes leads to the most unexpected people asking for some kind of spiritual help, which they would not have done if the Samaritan's attitude of trying to help the client to find what he himself wanted to be and believe had not inspired confidence in the Samaritan's integrity and unwillingness to exploit the client's vulnerable state of mind. The only preaching the Samaritans are allowed to do is in deeds, and if these do not themselves speak of love (which is the only unmistakable way to speak of God), then verbal puffs will not enable them to convey this message more clearly.

On one occasion in the early days (and my only excuse is that I was very tired) I slipped up on this, and told a client that God loved him. This was a silly thing to say, because although it was true, it could not possibly have appeared so to the client. Even allowing for exaggeration, he had had a dreadful life, and had every reason to suppose that if there were a god at all, this god had it in for him. He made a great show of staring into every corner of the room, and then said, 'I do not see this person of whom you speak. My senses tell me that you are the only person here with me. Do *you* love me?' I shall always be grateful to that client for reminding me that even those of us who realise that most of God's loving of people is done through other people, and have consistently taught this, may ourselves slip up if we are not constantly on the watch against blah. Of course, there are sometimes circumstances in which the client *wants* to be told of God's love, but these are few and far between; almost always it is *our* love the client must be assured of, and that not merely by stating that it is so if our whole attitude contradicts this.

When I say that we must preach only by deeds, I do not mean that it is always necessary to *do* something. I have already indicated that there are instances where simply listening and caring are what the client most wants. Rushing around in small circles in a vain attempt to give such clients 'practical' help would be to fail them. True love expresses itself by being attentive to the client in order to discover what it is that he needs from us that we can rightly give. Perhaps the *easiest* clients to help are those for whom we are able to do something, however much trouble it may be, whose beneficial results we can plainly see. It may be that the deepest and most effective help we give is when we cannot think of anything to do, and when we feel, after the client has gone, that we were not able to help him at all. If we have borne it all with him and now feel like a piece of chewed string, the chances are that the 'power that has gone out' of us has gone into him.

Those of us who pray at all, pray for the clients with whom we have dealings, but we never pray *with* them, except at their explicit request. With some clients, one senses that they would be disappointed if one did not say, 'God bless you' on parting from them, and once that relationship has been established with a client so that you know the kind of person you are dealing with, it may be possible to tell him that he is remembered in your prayers. Sometimes he is pleased by this because he thinks there may, after all, be something in prayer, and sometimes he is pleased because it makes him feel as though he were almost a member of your family.

Of the clients who do want some kind of specifically religious comfort, the majority wish to make a confession and receive absolution, whether formally in church or informally in the room in which they are being interviewed. For those who believe in God, confession and absolution is a most potent means of help and healing. Rightly used, and applied to theological and not to pathological guilt, the confessional can give great peace of mind and renewed hope. Wrongly used, it can increase people's feelings of guilt and unworthiness, and it is sad to find how often this has been the effect of previous confessions made by some penitents who come to Samaritan priests. Where a penitent has been taught to regard as his major sins things which are either minor or not sins at all, the confessor has to begin by revising the confession and putting things in their correct order. He also has to impress upon the penitent that there are no limits to God's patience and forgiveness. Most important of all, absolution must be absolute: 'Whosesoever sins thou dost forgive, they *are* forgiven.'

Befriending as a supplement to psychotherapy

Some clients have been able to be helped effectively in the confessional where psychological methods of help have completely failed, but of course the converse is true, and there are some whose feelings of guilt can only be dealt with by competent psychotherapy. Befriending seems to help in a supplementary way in such cases by providing the acceptance of an 'ordinary' fellow human as well as the acceptance of a professional, which the client may feel is part of the latter's professional equipment. The same is true of clients who are being counselled about the more recondite sexual deviations. The acceptance of them by the person doing the counselling is sometimes discounted to some extent on the ground that those who are dealing with such matters every day become inured to them and would not turn a hair at anything. But if they find themselves being befriended by somebody who possibly finds such aberrations incomprehensible and alien, and yet accepts them as part of the struggle of human beings who are coping, as all of us must, with their sexual needs as best they can, they cease to think of themselves as being beyond the pale.

Nobody could possibly envy those who are caught up in some compulsive activity whether it be a sexual deviation or drug addiction or a tedious obsessional ritual. Anyone who is under a compulsion to do things which mostly bring him little or no satisfaction is to be pitied, and deliverance from such compulsions is clearly not a matter of the person being confined in some moral strait-jacket, but a longed-for liberation. The approach of those who consider that other people's 'misbehaviour' is invariably a deliberate and conscious choice of forbidden delights is not only stupid and false, but has no chance whatever of being helpful to the person concerned. It also indicates unrecognised difficulties in the person who is adopting this attitude. We all of us have a tendency, which needs to be watched, to do two opposite things in relation to other people's behaviour, and particularly sexual behaviour: namely, 'compound for (i.e. make up for) sins we are inclined to by damning those we have no mind to' and also 'compound for sins we are inclined to by damning those we *have* a mind to'. For instance, some of the most vicious letters written to newspapers about the Wolfenden report on homosexuality when analysed carefully gave every indication of having been written by latent homosexuals, though others were equally clearly written by people who had been fortunate in their transition at puberty to heterosexuality and were completely lacking in the imaginative sympathy which permits one to understand difficulties one does not oneself experience.

Any Samaritan volunteer worthy of his membership soon learns the importance of Christ's command, 'Judge not, that ye be not judged; condemn not, that ye be not condemned; for with what measure ye mete, it shall be measured to you again.' Judging and condemning are such natural activities, so enjoyable to the natural man, that the Christian must regard the abandonment of them as a sign of supernatural power working in the person concerned, whether he would himself describe it in this way or not. Refraining from judging is not condonation, is not indifferentism, is not calling good evil and evil good; it is simply accepting one's status as a fellow of all other human beings, who are not to judge one another but are equally living under judgment.

One of the great problems is people who insist on judging *themselves*. They are often charitable towards other people, but towards themselves they are harsh. It is difficult to get them to realise that what appears to themselves to be setting a very high standard, if not a counsel of perfection, is in fact a great blasphemy arising out of deep spiritual pride.

Pride, and a sense of utter unworthiness, might appear to be complete opposites, and of course they sometimes are, but they are more closely connected than most of us care to admit unless we have considerable self-awareness and honesty. Relationships are therapeutic in so far as they encourage and increase these qualities. It is because the psychopathic and psychotic are not capable of insight that they are not amenable to psychotherapy, and because the neurotic find it so painful that a strong personality, loving and unsqueamish, is required for it, as well as skill and experience. The type of person who makes an effective Samaritan is similar. But so surgical an expression of this personality, essential for counselling, would be inappropriate for befriending, even if the befriender had the necessary knowledge. Psychotherapy, counselling and befriending are different functions, but the people who perform them in The Samaritans are all in their distinct ways Samaritan types, and they understand and value one another. For instance, psychiatrists who work closely with The Samaritans are themselves people who could be Samaritans if their professional function and duty did not disqualify them. It would be improper for people capable of giving medical treatment to employ their time and energies in befriending, which the lay person of similar calibre does at least equally well, and more acceptably to most clients because of the greater likelihood of common interests, and does so without danger of lapsing into professional detachment.

A Branch of The Samaritans ideally consists of people who are all truly Samaritans but whose function depends on other qualifications. Psychiatrists and other doctors, theologians, social workers, lawyers, etc., find themselves acting as Consultants, either advising the Leadership about clients, or seeing clients referred to them, or both. Parsons find themselves acting as Leaders, directing the activities of the volunteers and sharing in the work of counselling as far as they are able; whilst lay people only are normally accepted as volunteers to do the main work of befriending and interviewing. The cross-fertilisation between these three groups is of advantage to all of them, and, most important, to the clients.

Spread of the Samaritan idea

My idea of an emergency service for potential suicides received widespread publicity not only in the United Kingdom but also on the Continent and in other parts of the world. As early as the spring of 1954 a man who had read about me in a Greek newspaper hitch-hiked all the way from Salonika to see me; another man wrote from Havana, Cuba, about a very recondite sexual problem; and a man telephoned me in heavily accented English from Copenhagen saying he could only afford three minutes and how could he prevent a girl in his office from committing suicide? (I said: 'I don't need three minutes, just three words: stay with her.' He thanked me, and then asked 'But what if she wants to go to the toilet?' I told him: 'This is no time for prudery: don't let her lock herself in *anywhere*. As long as you stay with her, she's safe, and you'll find out what else you need to do.' I never heard what happened, but I am used to that.)

An article in a Swiss magazine described my work and also that of a man who for some months in 1954 advertised an Ilford telephone number for suicidal people to ring but then emigrated. The paper confused the two of us and attached his name to a photograph of me and some of my earliest volunteers, but at least the idea was publicised in German and attracted the attention of pastors who later started anti-suicide work in Hälsingborg, West Berlin and Zürich, except that the emphasis in these places at that time was on the ministry of an individual pastor—something I had already abandoned.

Although by 1954 The Samaritans was no longer a one-man band, I was kept too busy to make any attempt to organise similar services in other places, even in Great Britain. It is not surprising, therefore, that the centres which began operations a few years later on the Continent differed considerably from my original model, even though in some cases the organisers did not rely only on magazine articles for their information but also wrote to me for advice. To some extent, differences of method of working arise out of national differences, but these may easily be exaggerated: human beings are much the same everywhere, and most differences that still exist seem to me to arise from a different conception from that of disinterested 'Samaritan' help for the clients. I am not here concerned with the fact that most continental services work only on the telephone, often from secret addresses. There can be, and are, services working in entirely the true spirit of the movement who have not sufficient volunteers to be able to offer a 'walk-in' centre, or even to send a volunteer to meet a desperate client at an agreed rendezvous. The crucial question is not whether a service is able to allow the client freedom to choose between telephone and face-to-face encounter, but whether the service puts the clients' interests first. It is obvious that any service which, instead of choosing its members for their aptitude for the work, restricts member-ship to adherents of a particular religion or denomination, is going to be tempted to take the interests of that body into account. Even if it resists the temptation to proselytise or try to convert clients (and the fanatical don't know when they're doing it, so their denials are sincere), it will be suspect in the eyes of a majority of potential callers, and thus fail to meet the need.

It was not until 1959 that the second centre called 'Telephone Samaritans' was founded: this was appropriately in the northern capital, Edinburgh, on the initiative of the Rev. (now Prof.) James Blackie. The first centre in England outside London was started at Liverpool in 1960 by the then Rector, the Rev. Christopher Pepys, now Bishop of Buckingham. Our first centre in Northern Ireland was established in Belfast in 1961, and it was a great triumph for the Samaritan ideal that in a city where religious conflicts are so violent, the Director, the Rev. W. G. M. Thomson, a Presbyterian (who later followed me as Chairman of The Samaritans Inc.), was assisted from the beginning by an Anglican, a Roman Catholic and a Methodist.

Although I gave what help I could in the founding of new centres, both by correspondence and by paying visits when invited to do so, the demands of the work in London were too great for me to feel any temptation to try to set up actual branches of 'The Samaritans of St Stephen Walbrook', integrated with us and coming, however flexibly, under my supervision. It is now clear that this lack of correlation in the early sixties grievously delayed the unity now achieved in the UK but still unattained and probably unattainable overseas.

At that time I had my hands so full that I think I should have been unable to carry on had not the Calouste Gulbenkian Foundation come to the rescue in 1959 with a most generous grant, which continued for six years, to enable me to have

73

the help of a paid staff – something only the biggest cities require. One of them was the Rev. John Eldrid, who later succeeded Dr Thomson as Chairman (and was succeeded by Mr David Arthur, who had represented Scotland at Conferences as early as 1960.) It was hoped that I should be set free sufficiently to organise more and more centres, but a variant of Parkinson's Law increased the number of London clients to take up all the time of my staff and myself. It was not until 1963 that it became imperative to form an Association without any further delay, and the twenty-one centres in existence at that time banded together as Foundation Members of a Company Limited by Guarantee, licensed by the Board of Trade to omit the word 'Limited' from its title.

The founding Branches were Aberdeen, Belfast, Bombay, Bournemouth, Brighton (later discontinued, now replaced by Hove), Cambridge, Dundee, Edinburgh, Glasgow, Hong Kong, Hull, Jersey, Karachi (later discontinued), Liverpool, London, Manchester, Portsmouth, Reading, Salisbury (Rhodesia), Stoke-on-Trent and Woolwich (later discontinued). There were at that time in addition sixteen Probationary Branches and fifteen Preparatory Groups.

They differed considerably from one another in their traditions; but thanks to the Samaritan spirit they were able to weld themselves into a harmonious organisation within eighteen months, and the rapid spread of the movement and the improvements in our practice which have taken place since the Association was formed are the proof that this was a right, indeed overdue, step. The strength of the Association lies in its Branches, one of which is the original London centre, which is *not* the Headquarters.

The formation of the Association was prepared for by National Conferences, the first held at Balliol College, Oxford, in 1961, and the second at St Mary's College,

Durham, in 1962. In 1963, at Sheffield, we had our third Conference, the first since the formation of the Association. In 1964, we divided our Conference into Northern and Southern sections, at Dundee and Christ Church, Oxford, respectively, but in 1965 returned to the plan of one Conference for the whole country, at Manchester University. Since then the annual Conferences have been at Cardiff, Glasgow, Southampton, Keele, Exeter, Leeds and Stirling, and the annual Leaders' School was from 1972 duplicated, one held that year at Swanwick, and the other in the University of East Anglia. The eleven Regions into which the country is divided have their own Conferences at least once a year, and some of these have a very large attendance.

The papers which make up the second part of this book were mostly read at one or other of our Conferences, and two things are noteworthy about them. First, that the lay volunteers, who greatly outnumber Leaders and Consultants at Samaritan Conferences, find it natural that most speakers should be Samaritan psychiatrists and other experts; and secondly, that the lectures demonstrate both the differences of approach to the same subjects by the various lecturers, and the underlying unity of attitude amongst those closely associated with The Samaritans. Although The Samaritans has been forced to become an organisation, in order to serve more clients better, it is more like an organism, living and growing and developing. It refuses to become ossified, seeks harmony rather than uniformity, and is prepared to scrap even the oldest tradition and jettison any method proved ineffective in serving the needs of the clients. Only one thing is sacrosanct, and that is the task to which, and the spirit in which, we have dedicated ourselves: namely, to behave like the Good Samaritan in the parable towards those who are suicidal or despairing.

The mystique of the Samaritan method*

Richard Fox

There are essential differences between what I do as a consultant psychiatrist in the Health Service and what Samaritans do themselves. I am sent patients by other agencies, usually the family doctor, and seldom take them straight off the streets as Samaritans do. I have a letter of referral and often other documents which give the background of the disorder. Samaritans usually have nothing except what the client tells them, which may be accurate or may not. If someone wants to see me he makes an appointment (which may be weeks ahead) and will be at a place of my choosing. There are medical emergency services: the family doctor is contracted to supply them and can be fined for leaving his practice unattended, but not, of course, for being out on his rounds for a couple of hours. The family doctor can call the specialist urgently to a patient's home, but one may have other commitments.

These are important differences, and of course the Good Samaritan did not content himself with giving the injured

* From an address to the third International Conference of Telephone Emergency Services, Oxford, 1964.

traveller an appointment for the Jerusalem County Hospital for Friday fortnight at 2.45 p.m.

So the first part of the mystique is obviously instant availability.

The next major difference between us is what we do with our client or patient when he finally breaks through to us. He may go to the Samaritans for all sorts of reasons, but what they have to offer above all is *friendship*. He comes to me for advice, consultation, treatment. I am the specialist with my name on the door. The psychiatric patient bares his soul to me just as the medical patient bares his chest to the physician. Even if he is the local Lord Mayor, the patient is at a psychological disadvantage in that he is coming to me for help.

However informal one tries to be, this is a professional relationship and one does not take one's patients out for coffee, give them one's home telephone number (mine is ex-directory), write them little affectionate letters in one's own handwriting and make oneself available at all times of the day and night. The relationship may be warm, it may be intense, it may have all kinds of deep psychological meanings which have to be brought out and discussed, but the game is played according to fairly strict rules.

I do not say that friendship and a professional treatment relationship are mutually exclusive – rules are made to be broken – but it is the very exceptional patient and therapist who can handle such explosive possibilities. All this is far from the Samaritan mystique of befriending which *must not probe* into things the way the therapist does. To probe can represent 'psychological seduction' and can be a hazardous business. So Samaritans must realise that there are things that their method just cannot manage, just as I realise that there are plenty of things *my* method cannot manage. The lesson is that they and I must have a clear idea of what we are each trying to do, and not hesitate to cross-refer cases where necessary. The Samaritan mystique is in many ways more demanding than my own, though it calls less on training and more on broad human qualities.

One of the most crucial features in the Samaritan relationship is the acceptance by the befriender of negative, unpleasant features in the client. All of us have a nasty side buried – or not buried – somewhere, and troubled people who come for help will from time to time show attitudes or behaviour personally repugnant to the one who helps. The 'certain man' who lay by the side of the road when the Good Samaritan passed by was evidently not a pleasant sight, covered, one supposes, with blood, dirt and flies. And that is life. The Samaritan volunteer with pretty ideas of what clients ought to be like had better look for other forms of service. Introductory talks on sex to our prospective Samaritans are deliberately made rather nasty in places, and as expressions of horror pass over the faces of the more upright of the local citizens it is explained that though these things may be nasty, they exist, and sooner or later Samaritan workers will meet them. Repugnance against sexual deviation is common, but clients will feel they must unburden themselves of guilt about, say, homosexuality or paedophilia and any volunteer who feels unable to face this should realise that he or she ought not to be entering this work at all.

Sexual minorities are accustomed to ostracism to the point where they assume it when none exists – a paranoid reaction but based all too often on real and bitter experience. Any nuance of disgust or rejection in the befriender will be picked up, and the client may go forth in sadness thinking that the Samaritan is 'just like all the rest'.

The opposite error takes various forms. There is the be-friender (or therapist), for example, with ill-adjusted sexual problems himself who urges the client (or patient) into more and more elaborate accounts of all that he has done, with whom and how, getting thereby some vicarious erotic satisfaction. This is the lascivious 'Tell me more' approach, which is a form of voyeurism. Or there is the befriender who hastens to ill-judged reassurance, making light of a disorder which the client knows all too well is of the greatest gravity. Some acts are wrong when judged from almost any social, rational or religious point of view, and a befriender who says that they are not is being hypocritical and will forfeit the trust of his client. Or there is the befriender who thinks he can give support by baring his own soul in return. This is perhaps the commonest pitfall, and 'I have suffered too, old chap' approach. I do not say one must *never* do it, but I do regard it as fraught with danger.

To start with, the client has quite enough troubles of his own, without taking on another's. Then there is the risk that he will lose confidence in a person who is evidently as deeply troubled as he is. I learned my lesson over 20 years ago, just after qualifying, when I shared some rather personal confid-ences in an effort to relieve a young patient in much distress, but who then passed on everything I had said with much gusto to every nurse and doctor that she met. But Alcoholics Anonymous, and similar organisations, work, of course, on the basis that the members help each other by sharing their past experiences. The risk of mutually shared distress is probably much less great at the friendship level than in the patient/therapist situation. It is the counsellor who must particularly beware of going naked, as it were, into the vestry or consulting room.

Finally, there is the client whose unconscious motive is to

gain attention and fuss, to produce a shock effect, and who will plumb greater and greater depths of degradation – in a masochistic sort of way, perhaps – until he *does* produce some response in his befriender. One thinks of the good old days of the Salvation Army when the Alleluias mounted in enthusiasm as the public confession became blacker and blacker (and the hand-out afterwards became correspondingly larger).

What no Samaritan can expect, of course, is the reward which the client can offer by way of gratitude. It is nice when one's patient or client offers thanks, but rather uncommon. By and large people hate being ill, they hate having to go for help and putting themselves in a rather humiliating way into the hands of others. This hate often spills over, in the irrational way that the mind works, on to the person that they go to for help, and one must be aware always of this undercurrent of hostility – of ambivalent feelings – which can interfere with treatment. Or with befriending. Hostility is often part of the 'transferred emotions', again, formerly directed towards the parent or parent-figure: the 'negative transference', as we call it then. The Samaritan who has done a good job can expect a kind word from the Director. Any gratitude from the client is a bonus.

These are exceedingly difficult problems in which reading articles or listening to talks can act as no more than signposts. Every road has different, uncharted turnings, and learning to drive is a long and tedious business. Trial and error is one way of learning, but an instructor can often save one from going straight into the canal. The golden rule, in so far as there is one, is to be sympathetic but uncommitted, to listen with compassion but without judgment, and to avoid giving advice as far as possible, particularly when it is un-asked. It is *not* the Samaritan's job to tell the client to change his job, divorce his wife or invest in unit trusts. One must remember always the undercurrent of hostility. *Whatever you advise is likely to be wrong, and then it is your fault.* Samaritans, however, have been known to carry this to an absurd extreme of replying to a query: 'Sorry, I'm not allowed to give advice.' Better than this sort of brush-off is to help the client talk round his problem until he can see it in a clearer light and make his own decision.

Just as the young doctor must learn with sadness that he cannot cure everyone, so must the young Samaritan realise, without losing too much sleep, that there are those whom his mystique, however mysterious, cannot help, and that unskilled attempts to do so may rebound on both him and his client. The Samaritan Director and Psychiatric Consultant must keep in the closest touch with the befriender where predominantly psychopathic conduct is suspected. The main difficulty in recognising this is that psychopathic conduct shades off at all points of the compass into the normal. Clearly, we must not allow fears of the destructive psychopath to paralyse our efforts to help those who are on the fringes of the disorder.

One could, if one had the wisdom, talk endlessly of the pitfalls that await one in one's relationships with others – it is a book of life. Frankly, after seventeen years in psychiatry and six in other branches of medicine, plus six years of medical training, I know that I am still a beginner. Pablo Casals, surely one of the greatest cellists that ever lived, said in his eighties that he practised diligently every day and, he thought, continued to make progress. One can but try to emulate that.

Twenty principles of the Samaritans

Originally formulated and later revised by Chad Varah. Further revised by him at the request of the Council of Management, and approved by its Executive Committee on the 10th January 1973.

1. The Samaritans are a world-wide fellowship of volunteers dedicated to the prevention of suicide and the alleviation of the loneliness and depression that may lead to it, by making their befriending immediately available at any hour of the day or night to those who feel they have no one else to turn to in their distress.

2. The befriending which the volunteer offers to the caller is the personal concern of a compassionate fellow human being who, like the Samaritan in the parable, seeks simply to love him as a friend in his time of deepest need.

3. The volunteers are carefully selected for their personal qualities and natural aptitude for the work, without regard to their creed, colour, politics, age, sex or status.

4. The volunteers in each Centre recognised as a Branch of

The Samaritans work under the supervision of a Director (or Chairman) and other Leaders, who are advised by Consultants with medical or other professional qualifications, so that the highest standards of caring may be achieved. Consultants may also assist in the selection and preparation of volunteers and give help to clients.

5. In countries where the telephone is generally available, an easily remembered telephone number is advertised by each Branch, in addition to its address, to enable swift (and if the caller desires, anonymous) contact to be made with the minimum of effort on the part of the caller.

6. The Samaritans receive callers in person at their Centre, and invite telephone callers who seem likely to benefit to meet a Samaritan face to face. Callers are free if they wish to have contact only by telephone or by letter.

7. The Samaritans' primary and overriding concern is for those who seem to be in immediate danger of taking their own lives.

8. Samaritans engage in long-term as well as short-term prevention of suicide by befriending despairing and lonely people who do not seem to be suicidal at the time when they seek help, or who seem unlikely for conscientious or other reasons ever to commit suicide.

9. If a caller is concerned about another person, The Samaritans try to support him in his anxiety and to suggest ways of obtaining help for his friend. The Samaritans do not intrude upon persons who have not sought their help directly, unless an identified responsible person informs them of the need of someone who is too young or old or ill to ask in person, in which case they may make a tentative offer of help.

10. The Samaritans do not permit their immediate availability in cases of a suicidal emergency to be impeded by attention to cases of long-term chronic inadequacy, though callers in this category may be accepted as clients during a crisis.

11. The Samaritans do not flatter themselves that what they have to offer will be helpful to every caller. Those in charge of each Branch are responsible for using their human resources to the best advantage, and protecting them from being wasted by the grossly psychopathic or any others not capable of benefiting from befriending.

12. The Samaritans' service is non-medical. Callers requesting medical treatment may be helped to obtain this, and each Branch has at least one medical consultant, usually a psychiatrist, to advise those in charge of the Branch about such cases.

13. The Samaritans are not a trained case-work agency, and volunteers are not permitted to attempt to do for a client in an amateur way what social workers are trained to do with professional competence.

14. The Samaritans are not a social welfare agency. They refer those who request material aid to the appropriate welfare services, except in countries which lack these.

15. The Samaritans are not a Christian organisation, except in the origin of the concept. Volunteers, whatever their original beliefs, are strictly forbidden to make any attempt to convert the callers or to exploit a caller's distress by using the opportunity to witness to the volunteer's beliefs. Callers spontaneously requesting spiritual help of a particular kind are referred, with their permission, to a representative of the appropriate body, who may or may not be a member of the organisation.

16. Volunteers are normally known to callers only by their Christian names or forenames and their volunteer's indentification number, unless continued befriending by a chosen volunteer is arranged, when one of the persons in charge of the Branch decides what other information may be given to the client concerned and whether hospitality may be offered by the volunteer in his or her home.

17. The fact that a person has sought the help of The Samaritans, and everything he has confided in them, is confidential within the organisation. All communications from callers which could reasonably be regarded as of a highly secret nature, and those relating to criminal acts, are received in the strictest confidence and are revealed neither to any person outside the organisation without the callers' express permission, nor to persons within the organisation who are not involved, except the Director. Volunteers are not permitted to accept confidences if a condition is made that not even the Director should be informed of them.

18. The caller remains at all times in charge of his own destiny and is free to reject the help that is offered and to break contact without fear of being sought out against his will, even if it is felt certain that he intends to take his own life or to commit some other act which The Samaritans would deprecate. A volunteer in contact (whether by telephone or face to face) with a caller judged to be in some danger of suicide is encouraged to seek the caller's permission for a discreet approach to be made to him subsequently to ask how he is, and to record the fact if permission is granted. In such cases 'follow up' is clearly not against the client's will.

19. The various Branches of The Samaritans are banded together in a legally constituted Association whose Council of

Management represents all the Branches and reserves to itself the appointment of the person in charge of each Branch, responsible for seeing that the above-mentioned principles are observed.

20. Only the Council may authorise departures from these principles, for instance by permitting new Branches to offer a limited service for a period, or overseas Branches to use some other name; and only the Council may from time to time revise these principles.

International norms

International Federation of Telephone Emergency Services (*Version agreed on by the International Committee in its meeting at Cartigny on 30 March 1972 and carried unanimously by the General Assembly of I.F.O.T.E.S. at Geneva on 30 April 1973*)

A. Aim

To offer, while absolutely respecting the individual's liberty, to anyone in distress or despair, or contemplating suicide, the following possibilities:

1. Of establishing immediate contact with someone who is ready to listen and capable of starting and carrying on a conversation with him;

2. Of meeting in this way a friend who is ready to try to help the person in the situation in which he finds himself whilst the crisis lasts;

3. Of being put in touch, if he so wishes, with someone

who is competent to help him to find an answer to his problem.

B. *Principles*

1. Callers must be certain of absolute confidentiality. No information given by clients must go to any person whatever outside the organisation without the express permission of the caller.

2. Neither callers nor applicants to become volunteers shall be subjected to denominational, religious, political or ideological pressures.

3. Professional and voluntary workers will be chosen according to the standards defined in the Norms A. 1, 2, 3. They will be chosen above all for their human capacities of understanding and of compassion, on their sense of solidarity and, subsequently, after a careful assessment of their dispositions and aptitudes for the training and the work.

4. No financial or other obligations will be imposed on callers.

5. Members will not testify at law without authorisation from the caller and the person in charge of the post.

C. *Methods*

1. In each post, the team is composed of voluntary or paid workers. The volunteers play an essential part in the activities of the post.

2. The members are subject to the continuous supervision of one or several persons appointed for this purpose by the organisation.

3. The post must have specialists who can be consulted. These specialists can be members or non-menbers of the organisation.

4. In general the first contact is established by telephone. If the caller so wishes he can make contact by letter. If he wishes to meet a member face to face this meeting shall take place on a day and at a time agreed. It shall rest with the person in charge of the post to decide whether the caller shall see the member with whom he has spoken on the telephone, or another one. He shall also decide the place of the meeting. Both the caller and the member of the organisation have the right to anonymity.

5. The post shall offer a telephone service available for 24 hours a day.

6. The members shall be rigorously selected and carefully trained for their task. Their training shall continue as long as they are members. They will work as a team.

7. In principle it is the caller who establishes, maintains, breaks off and re-establishes contact. The organisation shall not concern itself with a client against his will. But it might find itself obliged to tell him that there was no possibility of helping him in the future.

8. Collaboration with other specialised services can be established with the caller's consent.

9. Welfare aid may be offered to callers in areas or regions where this kind of help cannot be offered by other services.

Born Samaritans

Chad Varah

We may think of the human being as being engaged in a perilous adventure, beginning its earthly pilgrimage when the baby arrives through the birth canal into this dangerous and frightening world, helpless and crying, dependent upon kindness and care for its survival. Generally speaking, most of us regard the infant human being as deserving of very tender care.

We need not here concern ourselves with what the newborn infant may bring with it in the way of memory of any previous existence. We may suspect that *if* it has been here before, it feels both a lust for and a shrinking from the flesh. We make ourselves very vulnerable when we take on this flesh, experiencing great delights and unbearable miseries. And, of course, there are in every age people who make life miserable for all those who come within their reach, and there are those who try to make life a little bit more endurable – indeed, if possible, happy and joyous.

So we begin life, if we are fortunate in where we are born, among people whose general feeling is that we should be gently treated. However, it isn't long before this changes.

The older we get, the more people expect us to live without loving consideration. They are concerned about what is due from us to them rather than the reverse. So we gradually find ourselves adapting to a world which probably holds some security and warmth within the family circle – though not for everybody – but which, beyond that, tends to be harsh and callous, if not actively cruel.

Looking back at our childhood, we can no doubt remember wanting to be adventurous, but simultaneously wanting a feeling of safety. We found ourselves with a sense of curiosity, seeking truth and joy, and often encountering painful experience; we had a sense of wonder and reverence, but as we grew older those feelings became deadened. Soon we found our eager selves cramped by the need to make our way in the competitive world and to earn our living.

We were lucky if the significant people in our lives gave us a feeling of reasonable self-esteem, an acceptance of ourselves as human beings, members of the well-known 'human race', entitled to have a place in the world, deserving the forgiveness and tolerance one is equally willing to give to others. If we have this temperament it is not something we have created; it results from our early heredity and environment. Not all are fortunate in this way. Some people have grown up apologising for their very existence; others believe the whole world should wait on them hand and foot or even worship them. There are many distortions of the human being that can result from experiences in infancy.

I look at the human being with human eyes, without dark or rosy glasses, and I see humans with all kinds of inbuilt prejudices and tastes and predilections. In later life, the person on whom these have been grafted or impressed will be praised or blamed for them, and in both cases unjustly, for neither praise nor blame is wholly deserved. Admittedly, we can gain insight in adulthood and live down many prejudices and broaden our vision, but this too depends on our coming into contact with civilising influences.

We who belong to the Samaritans are the lucky ones. In spite of our various failures we find ourselves recognisably human and gratifyingly (though sometimes excessively) needed, with loving colleagues surrounding us. We *owe* such service as we can give.

In any case, if we are truly Samaritans, we can't help giving a hand if we come across someone in difficulties. It seems to be almost a physical impossibility for us to pass by on the other side. Our business is probably no less pressing than that of the priest and the levite, but we can neither pretend not to have noticed the one who needs help, like the former, nor actually look at him and still feel no compelling compassion, like the latter. We have hardly any choice about 'doing unto others as we would be done by', and we are not always pleased to find ourselves 'lumbered' once again. We are not so stupid as to be unaware that willing horses tend to be put upon, and that we aren't fit to be let out alone, without someone to see to it that we keep our helpfulness within bounds. The more we can show healthy self-concern when off duty, the less grumblingly we shall do our work when we're out of sorts or it's more than we bargained for. We don't know whether the original Samaritan swore when he first saw the bandits' victim. What matters is that he did what the client needed.

The nature of a Samaritan

I might twist a quotation and say that Samaritans are born not made, but it would omit certain things. You need patience, because sometimes you have to listen to the same story over and over again from someone who is literally obsessed by their trouble. You must listen until the story begins to assume some coherence and the client is calm enough to put things into perspective. You need to be tolerant, and come to terms with the fact that your ideals and standards are not everyone else's. That your way of living may be right for you but not necessarily for others. That if they hold ideas different from yours, theirs may not necessarily be wrong and yours right.

You must be practically unshockable. We hear many tragic and sordid stories in the course of our work, and even though we may sometimes be inwardly appalled at what we hear – *this must not show*. A look of horror or aversion could be enough to send someone away to commit suicide. Sometimes we are the last resort. If we turn away in disgust then what?

LEILA WATERHOUSE

Answering the telephone caller

Let us look at the situation from the caller's point of view. Let us say I have a problem: a big one, with other smaller problems woven in. I have no one I dare trust with the knowledge of my problems; perhaps I am ashamed because I cannot cope, when other people appear to cope so well. One day, or evening, or in the early hours of the morning when I cannot sleep, I wonder about picking up my telephone and dialling 'that number', which I have seen in the Personal columns of the newspaper night after night.

Of course, I'm not sure just who they are, these Samaritans.

That is a hypothetical caller, but it must often be the sort of background to those odd calls which we may shrug off, and log as silent ones. Perhaps we forget, the longer we do

Samaritan work, that though *we* may gain in knowledge, the caller is still much the same as he was in the beginning, when somehow we felt closer to him.

I wonder where our callers imagine us to be. In an office, probably; but surely a little loo-like office, away from the bustle of other people, where the conversation can be one to one and really confidential. They would probably be appalled to discover that the emergency telephone is often in a large well-populated room. In a few Branches there may even be, horror of horrors, another person, be he ever so Samaritan, listening in.

Background noise should stop when the 'hot line' rings. Even the click of a typewriter can be off-putting, for the Samaritan who is struggling to hear an indistinct caller, and certainly for the caller, who stands to lose his comforting person-to-person image, and begins to feel that an 'organisation' has got hold of him.

Dare I mention the possibility that *who* is in the office can also have an effect on the telephone relationship? If we have a Samaritan-in-Charge who is super efficient, or gives the impression of expecting super efficiency – or if a Director is present and we feel – however unjustly – that we are being judged for know-how, then our relaxed manner will disappear, we shall become anxious to 'do well' – with the resulting off-putting 'efficient' tone, or 'clever' questioning.

It can be nerve-racking not to know, when we pick up the receiver, what sort of problems will confront us.

It may be a simple query about accommodation or finance. It may be a sex-starved man masturbating in a call box, wanting to shock us by intimate personal talk; or the wife of an alcoholic who has been keeping up appearances, perhaps for years, with her life getting steadily worse until she is beginning to wonder if it's really worth going on living. . . .

94

And what about that decision to call out the emergency squad? Of course, we must consult a Director first. But it may help for us to realise that the caller who hysterically demands that 'someone should come', and raves and weeps, can often be 'listened' into a state of calmness, while Flying Squad pounds its own ear. If a caller tells us that we are the only one who has ever really listened to him, isn't it terribly tempting to be beautifully flattered into feeling we know better than the more experienced person who has issued the directive that this is someone unhelpable by us?

Much more likely to be serious is the buttoned-up individual who 'doesn't really know why he bothered us', 'is not worth listening to', 'thank you very much but he will be all right'. This is often one who should set our warning bells a-jangle, whom we should try to get talking, and to whom we should be prepared to give quick and maximum support. For he's the one most likely to go quietly away, and in order not to bother anyone, make a neat and efficient end to it all.

DOREEN BROMBY

Counselling is really a relationship with a person

The counsellor's role in this client-centred setting is not to impose an outside answer, but to help the client to draw the curtains inside himself, to remove his own fears about himself and to see his own solution.

The counsellor's job, if this is true, is somehow to help the client to examine what his real feelings are about the alternatives which are facing him, about what he is afraid of in these alternatives, looking what he is afraid of in the face.

I want to emphasise that this kind of approach to counselling is not simply a discussion between the client and the counsellor about his problem. This is where it is so difficult to describe this process of counselling. A discussion about the problem would be simply intellectualising. The counsellor's role is to help the client to recognise and accept his *feelings* in the situation, not his thoughts – those have been running round his head for goodness knows how long before he came to you, and they have been no help to him at all.

People ask 'Isn't there any room for advice, or help, or information?' and so on. I think it is useful to distinguish between simply giving information in the form of facts or data, which the client may need to help him, and which can freely be given without interfering with the client's independence; and giving advice or offering opinions on what he should do or how he should behave, which is not so helpful, because the client usually already knows what he should do, but can't do it.

With young people who do not yet know what their potential is in a given situation, provided that it's done with the right attitude, and after a good deal of building up a relationship with the person, a certain course of action may be pointed out to them, simply because it hasn't come within their own potential; they have not considered themselves capable of it. We may need to help them grow in this way. This departs from the strict idea of counselling, because one becomes much more of a father figure at this point, but what's in a name? Here again, the question is, what is going to help the client?

ALAN INGLEBY

Sex calls

In no field is the impulse to reject so powerful as in that of sexual deviation.

The average housewife, I imagine, when receiving a phone

call enquiring after her sex-life or inviting her to extend same, would slam down the receiver with an expression of disgust. She would be badly shaken, and would dread lest the phone ring again. She would want to report it to someone, get the caller into serious trouble, so that the nuisance should stop for good and all.

Not so with the Samaritan helper. *She* must not be the first to hang up. I say 'she' advisedly, because male helpers do not get these calls. If a male voice answers, the caller cuts out immediately, and a Silent Call is registered.

Women are invariably the victims of these calls. And this produces an interesting reaction among the men in the Branch. They are outraged that the ears of young women should be thus sexually assaulted.

And this reminds me of how shocked I was, as a young medical student walking the wards, that dimpled nurses, looking innocent, pure, unsullied, angelic, and so on (little monkeys!) should have to mop up vomit and other disagreeable ejecta from the beds of smelly old patients. Why should they have to do it? The answer, of course, was that it was part of their job. If they found they couldn't take it, they could opt out of the nursing profession. Similarly, any Samaritan helper who is unduly shaken by a distasteful phone call has really no business to be a Samaritan.

I say 'unduly' shaken, because it invariably comes as a shock suddenly to get such a call: an excited aggressive male voice demanding some sort of satisfaction in four-letter words. How should the Samaritan respond? Certainly not by immediately hanging up with an expression of disgust. Certainly not by coldly inviting him to come along to the office for an interview with the Director: this would be a brush-off. Little Willie doesn't want a man. He wants a woman. How then?

Well, with great diffidence, because I have no first-hand experience of the situation (at either end of the phone) I'd say: Keep calm and good-natured. Above all, take your time. Don't get panicked by the chap's urgency. There's really no hurry. If he chides you on your silences, you can say, truthfully, 'I'm sorry. I was thinking.' If you can bring yourself to talk back to him in his own language, and refrain from playing back his homely little four-letter words in toffee-nosed clinical jargon, you will make far better rapport with him: which is the object of the exercise.

Keep reminding yourself that he is immured in a phone box and can do you no physical harm. Nor is he capable of charging round to the office to rape you. He is much more afraid of you than you need to be of him. He is terrified of women, and at the same time, tormented by his temporary sexual urgency, which is at bursting-point. His daydreams are of triumphant rapes and humiliations of the formidable creatures; but all he can do is to throw stones from a safe distance: anonymous abuse from a phone box, and usually obtaining physical relief from his tension by masturbating the while.

Love doesn't come into the picture. The idea of love between a man and his mate is beyond his concept – for him, the outcast. (Think of the fun and the warmth and the glory he is missing. Really, Little Willie is greatly to be pitied.)

Now he has taken a tentative step forward. Instead of masturbating in solitude, he is involving the female sex. He is aggressive and abusive because he is afraid and, like the temper tantrums of a child, his behaviour is to be read as a cry for help.

Now's your chance. He is attacking you in your most vulnerable area. Can you take it without flinching or disgust?

Can you make a relationship with him – a telephone friendship?

How? The same way as you do with any other shamefaced client: by accepting him as he is, dispelling his loneliness, and making him feel worth while.

Let there be no talk of his coming along to the office – yet. He would almost certainly funk it, cut the appointment, and put himself in the wrong – and realise it. Let him know he's welcome to ring you up when you are on duty at any time (unless there are special instructions about him).

There are those who doubt the wisdom of this line of action, and ask, 'Aren't we thus encouraging him in his capers?' I myself would say we were canalising them. Far better that he should ring up a Samaritan who can take it on the chin than some widow or maiden lady picked at random in the phone directory, with the possibility of GPO phone-tapping, police traps and arrest.

I think the same applies to the exhibitionist who comes to the office to flash his genitalia at you. Let's keep him out of serious trouble if we can.

GEORGE DAY

The Samaritan response to the sex-caller

We make a distinction between:

Befriendable sex-callers: those who can accept our offer of a relationship, and respond to it.
Unbefriendable sex-callers: those who can't.

We believe this distinction is more meaningful, and more in line with other Samaritan practice, than being governed by whether or not callers are seeking 'gratification'.

The implications of this are:

1. The offer of a relationship must be effective, and can start while responding to the sex talk. Since the sexually tense caller will be one-track-minded, relief of the tension ('gratification') may be an unavoidable preliminary to growth of the relationship.

2. All Samaritan women need to be prepared to cope acceptingly, though none should be required to undertake further befriending.

3. The latter will be reserved to a group who are willing and approved for the task, who meet for mutual support, sharing of experience, further study, and backing from people who are experienced in sexual counselling.

4. New volunteers must hear taped demonstrations during preparation, so that they can consider how to cope before a sex call happens to them.

5. Our aim is to channel sex-callers to members of the special group for befriending. This takes patience and perseverance, but it can be done.

6. Experience gained should be shared in the movement.

THE SAMARITAN WOMEN OF GREAT YARMOUTH
AND LOWESTOFT

The Samaritans as an organisation

Basil Higginson

The Samaritans do not like organisation. They tolerate only the barest minimum of circulars and committees, and anything else which might reduce their time spent with the suicidal and despairing.

They do not wish to join 'the establishment', and avoid, as far as possible, positions of public authority and honour. They do not form pressure groups on public issues such as hospitals, housing or education, though they respect those who courgeously fight in the public arena, and Samaritans as individuals are not careless of their political responsibilities.

The growth of The Samaritans is described elsewhere in this book. In April 1963 the then 21 Samaritan centres, including 4 overseas, banded together to form a Company Limited by Guarantee. The Samaritans are governed by the Memorandum and Articles then registered at the Board of Trade.

The organisation at present is as follows:

The Council of Management consists of one representative of each full Branch, elected by the Branch Committee. This person may or may not be Director of the Branch. The Council meets 3 times a year, and its most important job is to approve the persons proposed as Branch Directors. It ensures that no one can direct a Branch of The Samaritans without wholeheartedly accepting and practising Samaritan principles and methods. The Samaritans thus preserve their distinctive role as a listening and befriending service for the suicidal and despairing.

The Executive Committee of the Council of Management consists of representatives of each of the eleven Regions into which the British Isles are divided. They are elected by the Branches in the Regions, so that the Branches are represented on the Executive Committee as directly as possible. The Executive Committee also includes distinguished psychiatrists and other National Consultants who generously give their time. Similarly, each Branch has its own Consultants.

The Executive Committee meets every two months to carry on the business between Council meetings and to consider general questions of policy. It is responsible to the Council of Management, which must confirm its decisions.

In this way The Samaritans seem to have stumbled on to an organisation which is thoroughly democratic, but also capable of effective action.

The most notable improvement in the standards of listening and befriending has been due to the work of the *Regional Representatives*, who look after the Branches in their Regions, and also speak for these Branches at the Executive Committee. The Regional Representatives organise Conferences in their Regions and in districts within their Regions, and are 'guides, philosophers and friends' to the Directors of the Branches.

The Executive Committee have appointed *Visitors* to visit Branches regularly, and report on the work of the Branches with clients. The Visitors' reports, with those of the Regional Representatives, guide the Executive Committee and the Council of Management in recognising Branches and Directors.

National Office The Council of Management employ two General Secretaries and an Administrative Officer at a small house in Slough.* The Branches can and do contact this office at any time for information and advice, subject to the directives of the Council of Management and the Executive.

Publicity The Samaritans have the services of a National Publicity Officer who advises on national and local advertising, which is vital to clients.

Fund raising There is a National Fund Raising Committee, and each Branch is encouraged to find a volunteer Fund Raising Officer as well as a Treasurer. Many Branches have recruited 'Friends of The Samaritans' in their districts.

Finance Each Branch is self-supporting and also contributes an annual levy, of which the rate is decided by the Council of Management annually. The present rate is 6 per cent of the Branches' running expenses.

---

* 17 Uxbridge Road, Slough, Bucks., tel. 32713.

Laymen and professionals in suicide prevention

Roy Vining

The degree and type of support which we as doctors can offer does not always meet the patient's need fully. In the first place time is often an obstacle, either because we are in a hurry, or the patient feels a duty to be brief. In the second place the doctor-patient relationship is asymmetrical: the doctor gives structure to the interview, which is based on the fact that one party is seeking help and the other offering it, and on the further assumption that the help offered will consist mainly of advice and treatment. A meeting of this type typically ends with the issue of a prescription, and a desk remains between the two parties throughout.

In a counselling interview some of these features remain. The counsellor will give structure to the encounter, summing up what has occurred as a pre-arranged time limit is approached, and the relationship still shows some asymmetry, though it will be less directive, and the desk will be less in evidence.

For the lay helper, engaged in what the Samaritans call 'befriending', the situation is rather different. The fact remains that one party is seeking help and the other offering it, but the nature of the help that will be given is less clearly foreseen and the helper does not seek to take charge of the encounter. As the two get to know each other, and meet in different places and cirumstances like friends, and talk of shoes and ships and sealing wax, and cabbages and kings (and not just about the client's problems all the time), the relationship can become more symmetrical.

This provision of a close, extramural, and ideally symmetrical relationship lies outside the terms of reference of the professional helper in his professional capacity – and even outside his consulting-room he may find this style of helping so alien to his training as to be very difficult. Sometimes Samaritan clients after a short contact have turned to me and said 'You a doctor, by any chance?' – and have frozen up quite noticeably on discovering that I was.

It is therefore clear that for some persons in severe distress a doctor is *not* seen as an appropriate helper in their need any more than a priest is. A person may be aware of a need for some unspecified sort of help, and aware too that the need is not for treatment whether medical or psychological. To whom is such a one to go? Here, surely, is where the non-professional can legitimately function, and where he may do better than the 'pro'. But he must be aware that sometimes the 'pro' is needed, and that it may be dangerous for the client if the lay helper tries to go it alone.

To guard against this The Samaritans try to ensure that those chosen for the work are themselves stable, able to handle their own anxieties in the helping situation, and capable of listening with some insight into the feelings implicit in what they hear. For this we use interviews, role-play, case-discussion, and observation by experienced helpers during a period of six to eight weeks in preparation.

We try to teach them to spot psychological illness requiring medical help, especially depressive illness (it is surprising how difficult this can be). We try to give them some insight into the kind of factors which can underlie disordered relationships or behaviour, and unmanageable emotions, but we believe that they must not engage in insight-giving to a client unless they have had training in counselling too. We try to show them how to help without giving advice.

All contacts of helpers and clients are supervised by trained people; clergy, social workers, doctors. These keep in touch with those engaged in befriending and guide them, and see clients themselves, if necessary, in order to assess particular situations directly. Sometimes supervision is provided intermediately by experienced lay helpers; two heads are better than one, and no Samaritan works alone.

*   *   *

It is not dangerous for people to talk to each other about their problems. The person who shares his perplexities with one close and respected friend is more likely to be helped rather than harmed. If his needs exceed what can be afforded by the therapy of friendship the experience is more likely rather than less likely to encourage him toward expert counsel.

WILLIAM SCHOFIELD

The Director and the volunteers

W. G. M. Thomson

Directors can be wrong. Yet direction must be accepted by
volunteers. The Director must direct. He must not hesitate
to remove from a case a volunteer who is being wrong-
headed. A volunteer, who would not admit that a client was
a psychopath, although we had the advice of a psychiatrist,
and all the signs were there, was innocently becoming
dangerously involved with the client. The case had to be
taken out of her hands. She could not understand my fears
for her, but she accepted direction.

Within the fellowship of the Branch the Director must
have the courage to rebuke, suspend and expel where
necessary. He must not risk the clients' chances for the sake
of peace and friendship. He must not risk the Branch's or
the movement's reputation because he dislikes being unpleasant.

He will, if need be, consult his Deputies or the Companions; he may refer the volunteers for counselling to a
Consultant; but the decision must be his. He cannot hide
behind anyone else in dealing with unsatisfactory or careless
volunteers, or with volunteers who forget our principle of

confidentiality. The Branch is a fellowship, but it is a disciplined fellowship.

Take correspondence, for instance: volunteers must not be left free to write such letters as they please. All sorts of difficulties can arise. Two contradictory letters arrived with us from different members of another Branch. A volunteer on the untested story of a young man wrote a letter to a girl that almost caused the girl to be thrown out of home.

The Director has to administer the Branch. He has to meet clients. He has to represent the Branch at all sorts of bodies. He has to appear on television and radio and be interviewed by the Press. He has to do his own daily job. How then can he give so much time and thought to volunteers? I don't know, but I do know that the only hope the desperate client has lies in the type of volunteer he meets, when he comes to a centre.

Crisis

George Spaul

The Samaritans is one of the very few organisations able to deal with personal crises at the time of occurrence. Numerous organisations deal very effectively with special kinds of crisis, but the Samaritans offer a crisis service – which in availability and organisation is exactly what is required. Those who are professionally associated with the organisation work with it to increase the effectiveness of the advantages it has.

There are three types of crisis: 1. Biological; 2. Environmental; 3. Adventitious.

These classes are not clearly differentiated and often examples are mixed, but for clarity let us say:

1. *Biological crises* are inevitable in the nature of man:
   Growth crises – e.g. weaning and puberty.
   Illness in general (none of us can hope to escape illness).
   Loss of function through age.
   Pregnancy and childbirth.
Biological crises because inevitable *should* be prepared for

through an enlightened education which would reduce the impact of biological crises, making the successful resolution almost universal. This is not yet the case.

2. *Environmental crises* are not quite so inevitable. In this group the whole area of personal relations is involved in the production of crisis:
Bereavement
Marriage
Retirement
Migration
In this class there is often an element of personal choice, and always a relationship involved. It is the area with which psychiatrists and Samaritans are most involved.

3. *Adventitious crises* are basically due to unlucky chance:
Injury
Unemployment
Disasters – flood, fire, earthquake, famine, etc.

Crisis resolution
The process of *crisis resolution* has been studied in detail, particularly in terms of disaster and migration, but the work done in these circumstances is also applicable to the more individual crises with which we more commonly deal.

Clinically there is one characteristic of the whole period of crisis resolution and it is so important that almost all writers and original researchers comment on it. It is the *openness of the personality* at these times. There are fewer defences (in psychological terms) and the personality is vulnerable from without. Intervention can be effective which is quite impossible at other times.

I speak of the whole personality – not just of the cluster of ideas or feelings involved in the actual events of crisis.

However, there is a very special responsibility about our intervention in a crisis – intervention *must* be restricted to relevant matters. It is possible to convert or unconvert a person much more easily during crisis resolution because the general defences of the personality are low. It is not accidental that 'brain washing' techniques have as their basis the artificial production of crises.

We have a special responsibility not to impose our brand of political, religious, psychiatric or sociological dogmatism on our clients when they come to us for quite other reasons. I know that this is laid down in Samaritan principles but it stands repeating, as does the idea that one can all too easily convert one's clients to 'Samaritanism' or to that particular form of idolatry which in psychiatry we call Transference Neurosis.

To return to *Crisis Resolution* – there seem to be *three phases* involved in the resolution of crisis:

1. Physical and mental *turmoil*
   Aimless activity or immobilisation
   Disorganisation of some degree – often great

2. *Painful preoccupation* with the past
   In psychiatric terms the person may *regress* to infantile or childhood methods of dealing with the world and with oneself. These methods include dependency, alcoholism, depression or withdrawal. If he finds these old methods either not workable in terms of a solution, or not acceptable in terms of his self-esteem, he may then go on to the third phase.

3. *Remobilisation*, activity, adjustment

> To simplify:
> Pain, digestion, action or
> shock, grief, action

It appears to be established that missing any of these phases leads to non-resolution, i.e. injury on a more or less permanent scale.

Problems are less painful than crises; they involve no disorganisation. No new solution (in terms of the personality) has to be found – it is merely a matter of sorting out already acquired functions and selecting an appropriate one.

Crisis presents pain and disorganisation and its resolution demands a change in the view of, or a readaptation to, the world, or the person – or both.

We have to allow clients *time* to get through the phases. Aid can only be effective in the second or third phase. We may need to protect the client during phase one.

Ego growth (increase in 'self-ness') can only occur during crisis resolution. A crisis successfully met leaves the person larger, more efficient, more capable than before – and permanently so. This underlies the necessity for the *solution to be found by the client*, not by the counsellor. If we ignore this: 1. we deny the client the possibility of growth; 2. we court dependency – non-resolution and regression to 'Daddy make it better'. It also explains why only *listening* is necessary on so many occasions, and why Samaritan volunteers are so valuable in this work.

Depression

Charles Bagg*

Depression is a many headed monster. We shall consider two of the forms in which it occurs.

Endogenous depression

The first depressive syndrome (i.e. collection of symptoms) that I will mention is ENDOGENOUS DEPRESSION. 'Endogenous' means generated from within. Endogenous depression essentially comes from within the person, not as a result of external misfortune.

The practical implication of this is that if you have got somebody with an endogenous depression, *don't think that you are going to make it better by tinkering about with the environment*, or *even by befriending them*. It is a condition which is not primarily and predominantly due to external factors, and it is not going to be remedied by external factors. If you fail to recognise that, and try to do your stuff on behalf of the patient, sooner or later you are going to put your foot in it, and there may be a very tragic outcome. This I have seen happen, not with Samaritans but in other circumstances.

* From a talk given at Samaritan National Conference 1969.

The answer, when you have diagnosed an endogenous depression, is to get it off your hands. Now by that I don't mean jettison the patient in an unkind way, but seek professional advice, and don't try to cope with the situation yourself. If you do and thereby fail to ameliorate the condition, the patient may commit suicide. Not everyone with endogenous depression will commit suicide – most of them don't, but it is a condition in which suicide is a known risk.

There are other unfortunate sequels – there will be a great deal of unhappiness that the individual will suffer, quite unnecessarily, because this condition is eminently curable. The unhappiness will be both for the individual patient and for the family. There will often be misunderstanding by the family, and when the family finally recognise with hindsight that the condition was in fact an illness, they will reproach themselves accordingly.

Loss of employment is another risk. The incompetence that this illness creates in individuals is liable to give them a reputation that they may not be able to live down, even after recovery, and they may, in fact, lose their jobs. Another thing that tends to happen is *marital disturbance*, and even, occasionally, a marital break-up. The depressed patient becomes very unattractive, and the marital partner, not understanding the reality of the situation, may construe the change as a loss of affection, and may go and seek affection elsewhere. For all these reasons it is important that this condition is diagnosed in the very *early stages*.

Usually when a patient comes to a GP, and still more to a psychiatrist, things have gone manifestly awry. Before that stage has arrived, any of these circumstances that I have just named may have developed, including suicide. *They may commit suicide before they ever get to the doctor.* Furthermore, anybody except a half-wit can diagnose endogenous depression in its advanced stages, in its clear cut form. To spot it in its incipient stages is a very different matter, and this is just the point at which you are likely to come in.

Endogenous depression comes on for no apparent reason, or if there is an alleged reason, that reason is in fact more apparent than real. Sometimes, I must admit, this illness does seem to have been genuinely precipitated by some factor, but this factor is only something that has just been the last straw, **it is** not the essence of the condition.

The symptoms of this condition are, first *a decline in interest and initiative and emotional response*. Matters which had previously been of interest to the patient cease to form the centre of his attention. Work or domestic duties are liable to tail off. A degree of incompetence, which may not be recognised as pathological at that stage, begins to assert itself. The patient begins to spoil his daily work, not necessarily very grossly, but to people who are working closely with him it becomes apparent. Often people cover up for him, because he is usually a very nice person who has always been very conscientious.

Since this illness tends on the whole to come on the basis of a conscientious personality, the sufferer tends, with commendable stoicism, to struggle against the illness. In the early stages he often succeeds, and this obscures from the bystanders the fact that there is an illness at all. The patient will feel different, he will feel this coming on, but you may not notice it very much.

Another feature is *indecisiveness*. The person who previously had been at least capable of taking firm decisions – though he often tends to have been the sort of personality that rather laboriously weighs the pros and cons – will become indecisive. This, of course, is a thing that often gets under the skin of people working with him, and gets under the skin of the marital partner; and to the misfortune of his illness is added the misfortune of recriminations.

All these things are part and parcel of 'Psychomotor retardation' – which is exactly what it says – slowing up of the psychological processes and movement. In the extreme stage of this condition I have seen people so frozen that they have been brought into hospital on a stretcher in a condition that is known as depressive stupor – they just can't move. It is seldom that one gets to that stage, but in a moderately severe case they often present a picture rather like a film in slow motion – with droopy stance, depressive facial expression, and slowing of mental functions. This is very distressing to them, and they find that they have to make a conscious intentional effort to drag out of themselves thoughts which, before they became ill, would arise perfectly spontaneously. Their concentration tails off, they will tell you that they read the paper and at the end of it they don't know a word of what is in it. As the condition gathers momentum, they can no longer overcome the disabling influence of these symptoms and they are laid low by the illness; at that point they go to the doctor – if they haven't committed suicide before.

All these symptoms, characteristic of the early stages of the illness, may very well occur without the patient spontaneously informing you of the facts. He is not the sort of person, normally, and still less when he is ill, who wears his heart on his sleeve, and he just won't tell you these things. So *ask him* whether he is getting indecisive, ask him whether he is losing interest; if once you suspect the diagnosis don't just leave him to tell you, because he may very well not do so, and you will have missed the significance of the whole thing.

There are certain qualities of thought which are extremely

characteristic of this condition and the cardinal feature, I would say, is *self-reproach*. He will blame himself, quite irrationally, for things which superficially might have a basis in reason, but which in fact are rooted in illness. This is where your skill in distinguishing between the two has to come into play – he will accuse himself irrationally of things, and in the gross degree of the illness the patient will say something which is so clearly delusional that nobody could possibly fail to recognise that he is in fact ill.

A delusion by definition is a false belief that is not amenable to reason. It is not founded in logic and it can't be dispelled by logic. So that if you try to use a logical approach, which would seem on the face of it the sensible thing to do, you are going to do no good at all, you are going to make things worse. Another delusion that is common in greater or lesser degree in this condition, is the *delusion of futility*. He feels, in the extreme anyway, that everything is utterly black, there is no hope, there is no salvation. Again, if you don't recognise the essentially morbid origin of this, you are liable to try to talk him out of it.

There may be delusions of *hypochondriasis* – that is to say, believing that there is bodily disease when in fact none exists. Such delusions are very characteristic of the depression of middle life and the senile period. They are very characteristic indeed of the menopausal depression, the involutional depressions (what used to be termed involutional melancholia), which occur in middle-aged women at the change of life.

Involutional melancholia is characterised typically by very bizarre hypochondriacal delusions, for example, a lady with agitated depression, who believed that her gullet stopped 'here' – I don't know what she thought happened to the food after that. This was one of the hypochondriacal delusions of involutional melancholia.

A further example, particularly characteristic in the senile period, is delusions of *poverty*. One has seen people, who are unquestionably well off who believe absolutely that they are financially ruined.

Loss of appetite is another very characteristic depressive symptom. They go off their food, or, even if they don't actually reduce the intake, they don't enjoy their food as they did. So this condition, anorexia, is very characteristic indeed of depressive illness.

Associated with this is loss of *sexual appetite*, loss of sexual interest, sexual capacity, sexual enjoyment, and of course this symptom tends, as you can imagine, to feed into the depressive tendency to self-reproach. They tend to feel that they are letting their marital partners down, and the marital partner may in fact feel rejected.

One more symptom that you really need to commit to memory is *insomnia*. This doesn't mean that because we sleep badly we have got depression, but there is a certain pattern to this insomnia which is characteristic of depressives. They wake during the small hours of the morning, only to be tormented with this ceaseless round of delusionally coloured unconstructive ruminations, as a result of which in the small hours of the morning they may get up and go downstairs and 'take a bottle', and that's the end of that.

Diurnal variation means that they are typically worse first thing in the morning. As the day goes on the condition improves.

There are certain phases in which *suicide* is a particularly high risk. Paradoxically, it is not so much when they are utterly immobilised by depression that the risk is highest, but when they are *going into the depression* – that is when you may come into it – and when they are *coming out of it*. When the depression is maximal, they are so retarded as to be incapable of the initiative, mental and physical, to make a suicide attempt. But give them three or four electric treatments, for example, and they are comparatively better, but they are still deluded and wretched; they are capable by then of taking the suicidal action, and this is the time when it is likely to happen. Also, when they are first going into the depression, particularly if they are receiving any form of anti-depressant treatment as out-patients, and are not under immediate observation in hospital – this is the time when you need to be particularly vigilant.

One feature of unmixed depression is that it can be satisfactorily cured, dispelled. I still never cease to wonder at the metamorphosis that one produces over three or four weeks or less in these cases. It is a condition, most often, from which they completely recover. The immediate outlook is very good, and there is no residual defect, but it is an illness which tends to recur. (So if you know of anyone who has had such an attack, just keep on the look-out for recurrence, and nip it in the bud.)

The person who becomes depressed is often an *obsessive personality*. Many of us are normally obsessive about details, about order, about tidiness, but an obsessional personality may develop a psychosis in which the person loses touch with reality and suffers from delusions – he does not understand that he is ill, but believes that he is guilty, useless or unclean.

FEATURES OF ENDOGENOUS DEPRESSION: psychomotor retardation, indecisiveness, self-reproach, the sense of futility, hypochondriasis, delusions of poverty, loss of appetites, the pattern of insomnia, diurnal variation; and the dangerous phases, going into the depression and partial recovery.

Reactive depression

By contrast, reactive depression is explicable and comprehensible in terms of the circumstances that preceded its onset. That is to say, if someone suddenly loses all their stocks and shares, they may go into a reactive depression. The condition subsides when these precipitating circumstances are resolved.

If, on the other hand, it so happened that an endogenous depression followed, perhaps precipitated by a financial disaster, it would not make one scrap of difference if I won all the football pools.

So you can spot the reactive depression, partly by a process of exclusion. You don't typically find it preceded by an obsessional personality, you don't find the diurnal variation, you don't find many of the other symptoms of endogenous depression; and they are not concerned primarily and predominantly and fundamentally with self-reproach, futility, hypochondriasis, etc. – they are preoccupied with whatever misfortune brought on this state. They are not typically retarded in the way that the endogenous depressive is. Indeed, if you have a co-existing element of hysteria in the condition, as you fairly frequently do, you will find that there is a flamboyant display of grief quite often.

There is no denying that they are depressed, but it is a different quality, it has a different essential origin, different management, and a different outcome. The chap who is displaying his grief may make an intentionally unsuccessful suicidal attempt, and get people terribly rattled, and get your name in the paper, but he is usually much less likely to land up in the tomb than the patient with endogenous depression.

The content of the reactive depression does not spread

into the irrational ideas which characterise the endogenous depressive. In the reactive depression, when once you are satisfied that this is what you are dealing with, don't be afraid of helping them in their crisis.

*   *   *

Role of the Samaritans in the management of depression

While acknowledging that severe depression is treatable with drugs, there are other ways Samaritans can help the sufferer.

One can be friendly, show interest, and give support: all this is helpful in all types of depression, but sometimes one has to realise that in severe depressions this may not produce very much in the way of an improvement. Nevertheless it is still important and still appreciated by the patient and he will remember it with gratitude later. It is important not to urge him to pull himself together, particularly when he is severely depressed, because he cannot do anything about it at that stage. As he gets better he will automatically find it much easier to do things and the need for encouragement will not be so great; but it is an appropriate time for encouragement to return to normal activities.

For the patient who has undergone treatment and is discharged home, it is often a critical time when commonsense and enlightened help with the patient and with his relations is so important. One has to try and live in the boots of one and the shoes of the other. Consider the patient first – he may still have some residue of his illness, he may have some feelings of inferiority and alienation as a result of his hospitalisation. He may have practical problems with re-employment. Consider the family, with their complex attitudes towards the patient's recent illness – there is often bound to be some apprehensiveness and concern for his future, some exasperation, perhaps, with any residual symptoms.

Bearing these principles in mind, befriending by Samaritans can provide invaluable help in one of the most distressing and incapacitating illnesses which afflict mankind.

W. LINFORD REES

The incurable case

As in other fields of medicine, psychiatry is still frequently faced with the incurable and untreatable problem. Depression is no exception in this field. There are some forms even of endogenous depression that do not fully recover after the most skilful and generous use of physical methods. This may be because of an underlying and insidious organic change such as cerebral arteriosclerosis, or it may be because of an admixture of some other mental disorder such as schizophrenia or hysteria, or it may be some as yet undiscovered biochemical abnormality. And then again with the reactive and neurotic forms of depression one must accept that there *are* insoluble practical problems in life which even the most devoted doctors or social workers are unable to ameliorate. The aim must then be to support the patient with the shared knowledge of their difficulties, but it cannot be pretended that the depression is being alleviated.

P. W. W. LEACH

'Masked' depression

Why is it that so many people, having consulted their general practitioners and even psychiatrists, almost straight away go off and still kill themselves? The answer, or a very large part of it, lies in the existence of large numbers of states of '*masked*' *depression*, which need special psychological training and skills to recognise. Doctors, whatever their philosophical viewpoint, do not in practice stand aside and let patients kill themselves, if it can be avoided. Yet thousands and thousands do either attempt or succeed in doing so each year, often with the very drugs prescribed by their doctor.

Let us get down to the basics of this problem. Around one third of the patients coming to St Thomas's, for instance, for various tests, X-rays and other physical examinations, are people of often sterling worth, who have worked regularly, supported families and relatives, helped others and been, in all respects, model citizens. Then gradually, or suddenly, they start to feel a variety of pains, sometimes in the head, or in the back of the neck. They may also complain of dryness of the mouth and throat. Their chest or heart may pain them periodically, or their stomach starts to get a vague tense and uneasy feeling. Constipation can be a major worry, or faulty eyesight, not helped by glasses.

Along with the development of these physical symptoms and abnormal feelings, they may start to experience intolerable anxiety for no known reason. Perhaps they have been through a period of stress which is now passing. They also start to become very tired for no known reason, or they may start waking early and regularly for the first time in their life. Some alternatively sleep deeply all night and still feel just as abnormally tired the following day, when they try to do their normal work. For many, jobs that were easy for them for years start to become difficult. Making decisions over simple matters also worries them. They become more irritable with people they really love, and later they may start to blame themselves for the most foolish things, and search their past lives for causes for self-blame.

When asked whether, in fact, they are depressed, they will generally say they are more tense and anxious. And they almost invariably attribute their increased anxiety to the recent onset of the physical symptoms, of which they are now complaining, and what these symptoms may portend, such as brain tumour, stomach cancers, coronary heart disease and the like. And it is then, to find out about these symptoms in somebody usually so well, that the patient is sent for special tests to a teaching hospital or elsewhere.

It is now that a mistake can be made by general practitioners, physicians and psychiatrists alike. This is to examine the patient very carefully, perhaps do all sorts of tests and X-rays and then tell him that he is normal and there is nothing very much the matter with him. Perhaps, even worse, is to say it is 'all nerves', which means nothing serious to too many doctors and patients, and to simply prescribe sedatives.

What is such a man or woman then to do?

They begin to think the only thing they can do, as they become more and more incapacitated and yet supposedly medically quite well, is to put themselves out of the way, to stop, by committing suicide, being a 'medically well' total burden to their family and themselves. How many patients, with a missed depressive illness, have gone to their death with their doctor's supposedly heartening reassurance, in their ears, that there is nothing the matter with them that a bit of will-power won't put right?

WILLIAM SARGANT

Clinical treatment of depression

1. *Drug treatment*

In recent years, psychiatry and general medicine have become equipped with two groups of powerful and effective drugs, almost specific in certain states of depression and anxiety. If general practitioners could learn their skilled use and not be too worried by side effects that happen with all powerful and effective drugs in medicine as a whole, they could themselves cope with around 75 per cent of the anxiety states and depressions in persons of adequate personality, without any need to refer them for specialised psychotherapy and psychiatric treatment. Several practitioners have already found this out, having taken the trouble to learn about them.

Drug manufacturers tend to claim that their particular anti-depressant drug covers the whole group of depressed patients, and muddle doctors up a lot with their excessive claims. There is a tendency to rush from one new anti-depressant to the next new one, although they may be the same group of drugs under different trade names. The two main groups of drugs must be discussed since too many people think they overlap where a few patients made worse by one are made better by the other and vice versa. The MAOIs (Monamine Oxidase Inhibitor drugs) are extremely valuable in states of anxiety and reactive depression in patients, who may have been ill for years, but are still fighting their symptoms. They are particularly valuable in phobic anxiety states, where people get panicky at going into the street, attending church or cinema, and going in trains, etc. These people are also depressed and can be suicidal in their despair about their restricted life. The MAOIs are also valuable in fatigue states, where people sleep deeply all night, and wake up just as tired in the morning, as opposed to those who wake up early in an extremely agitated state. Unfortunately, the MAOIs require certain dietary restrictions, and severe headaches when the wrong foodstuffs are taken frighten some doctors and patients off them. Nevertheless, unless they are fully used in states of depression, large numbers of people will remain ill, and possibly suicidal, since the MAOI responding depressions and anxiety states do badly with the other group of anti-depressants called the *tryciclics*. These are much more useful in patients who are retarded and slow with early waking and guilt. In fact, the 'masked' depressions often do best with the MAOIs, and the obvious melancholias with the tryciclics. And there are other neurotic depressions, who do best of all when both groups are combined. This is now quite safe if certain precautions are taken.

People have such silly attitudes to mental illness and drugs. Few would think it wrong to take insulin for diabetes or Vit. B12 for pernicious anaemia – both killing diseases. Yet some baulk at using drugs in depressive illnesses, which can be just as lethal, judging by the 50,000 to 80,000 suicidal attempts each year. One of the important things about the anti-depressants is that there is no need to increase the dose despite years on them. And please do not encourage patients to try to 'get down to the root' of their problems, when they are depressed. Lots of depressive illnesses are inherited, run in families, occur for no known reason, and respond to drugs: we do not yet know why. Such a position is common in medicine, where we do not know even how aspirin works. *Psychological probing can be very dangerous in depression.* Wait until the patient is much better with drugs or other treatment, and then see if he can be further helped psychotherapeutically without risk of precipitating a suicide attempt by trying to uncover material the patient just cannot cope with. ECT is a much older treatment than the new drugs. But there are still many suicidal depressives who will quickly get well with it, even when the drugs have failed to help.

WILLIAM SARGANT

2. *Electrical treatment*

The sheet-anchor in all forms of serious *endogenous illness is electrical treatment.* This entails the passage of a measured amount of current for a measured time through the frontal region of the brain while the patient is asleep with short-acting anaesthetic and muscle-relaxants given by the vein. One treatment lasts about three minutes and the patient is awake and up and about again in half an hour. Out-patients are able to return home and resume work on the same morning. About six treatments given twice weekly are sufficient. There are no ill-effects other than muzziness or headache for a period after each treatment and minor disturbances of memory lasting for a few weeks after a course of treatment.

P. W. W. LEACH

Many lives could be saved by a *more widespread recognition oj depression* in its many diverse clinical forms. There are many good treatments now for all sorts of depressive illness, especially if the previous personality has been adequate, which is so often the case in those making serious suicidal attempts. For faith in the value of treatment may not cure the patient, but if he trusts you he may postpone a suicidal bid till such treatments have been given a chance to help. And lots of patients will be helped by them.

WILLIAM SARGANT

Research on depressive illness

What are the particular symptoms of depressive illness that characterises the suicide? From my own experience of doing psychological autopsies, I think prolonged insomnia, months and years of it, and complaints of bodily symptoms are most common. Other helpful indicators are fantasies of the method of suicide, convictions of sinfulness, previous histories of suicide attempts, and situations of crises without social support of any kind; particularly married people separated or single people in middle life who have been bereaved of the parent with whom they were living.

The idea of the humoral origins of melancholia, that is that something was wrong with the body fluids, has an ancient history and was believed by Greek physicians. The Christian church has a bad record here, having fostered the idea of demonic possession as the explanation, instead of encouraging the more rational humoral theories. I believe the history of the Church's encounter with madness is responsible in part for the mistrust some psychiatrists feel in their relations with the Church.

Recently the Professor of Psychiatry at Edinburgh University said in his opening address to the World Federation of Mental Health conference, that belief in possession by the devil no longer existed in this country. But I recently encountered a woman with a lengthy history of manic depressive psychosis who towards the end of her life became deluded that she was possessed by a devil. She worked for two pious ladies who also believed this and prayed with her for relief. They informed me that her cure lay in exorcism. They also informed me that a minister of religion to whom this lady periodically resorted for prayer and healing also believed it, and had told her not to bother with any more electrical treatment, because that was not the way where healing lay.

The technical methods for testing humoral hypotheses are now available, and they have revealed some interesting differences between the body fluids of depressives and non-depressives. Melancholia being regarded (rightly or wrongly) as a brain disease, the crucial experiment of looking at depressive brains has to be done on dead depressives, and the easily available source is those who have died by suicide.

This enquiry was carried out recently at the MRC Neuropsychiatric Research Unit at Epsom. Dr Shaw looked at the brains of a series of suicides from London, separating them clinically into alcoholism, severe depression, and mild reactive depression on the evidence supplied by inquest notes. He looked at two aspects of the bio-chemistry, first the concentration of the salts of sodium potassium that maintain the integrity of the brain cells as electricity producing systems, and second the concentration of nitrogen-containing chemicals that are responsible for the transmission of the electrical stimulus from one brain cell to the next. He found distinct differences between the three clinical groups which in general fitted in with current theories about what happens in the brain during a depressive illness, and how the anti-depressant drugs work.

B. M. BARRACLOUGH

Causes of psychiatric disorder

Psychiatric disorder is not uniformly distributed throughout the population. It occurs in pockets. It occurs in certain sections of society more than in others. It appears to be more prevalent in some conditions in women than in men. It is certainly more frequent in the elderly than it is in younger categories and it may be possible in time to throw some light on to problems of causation, because this is a field where we are at the present time sorely in need of information. We know a certain amount about the cause of mental disorder. We know also how very ignorant we are on this matter. And we have to use all kinds of methods to forward this aim of discovering the causes of psychiatric illness: the clinical method, the bedside method, methods derived from the basic sciences, chemistry, physics, physiology and so on. The epidemiological method is one of these tools which we have and which we can use for this purpose, because if we can find certain sections of society, certain kinds of people, groups of people who have high rates for specific mental disorders and, conversely, if we find people who have low rates for these conditions, we may be able to derive clues about the causal factors operative. For example, it has been known for many years now that the prevalence of the psychiatric disorder schizophrenia, which is a serious condition, is highest in the unskilled section of society, what the Registrar-General calls 'Social Class V' – far higher in the members of Social Class V than it is among other social categories of the population. At first it was thought that this might indicate that something about the way of life in Social Class V was productive of schizophrenia. We now know that it is more likely that the high prevalence of schizophrenia in Social Class V is a consequence of the disease rather than a cause, because if you develop schizophrenia you may become socially less competent, you may lose your job, which may be a skilled job, and you may slide down the social scale. By the time you enter a psychiatric hospital, or by the time you become a declared case as it were, your social position may be that of an unskilled worker and therefore this produces an apparently high prevalence in Social Class V. This is an example of the difficulties which the method presents, the problems of interpretation which one has to cope with in using this method, and there are many such problems to be met and sorted out before we can really gain the maximum use from this method of enquiry.

KENNETH RAWNSLEY

Social pressures towards suicide

Everyone must pay homage to the new god which is called *efficiency*. More money must be earned by more work until everyone is pushed to the very limit of his tolerance. . . .

Workers pushed to the limit of their tolerance no longer conform to the principles of economic theory; they are no longer reasonable. When they strike, they are not crying for help: they are telling you that the conditions of life are intolerable. From animal studies we know that when the breakdown of social order begins it may progress with fantastic speed. We are witnessing today the early stages of the breakdown of civilisation in the most highly developed countries. It is the result of too many people and too great a drive to reach too much affluence, in short, too much competition. If life is to be made more tolerable we must have a dramatic reduction in the population: we must reduce considerably the competition in schools, colleges and universities: we must include some degree of inefficiency in every job carried out by a man or woman: we must be content with less affluence.

IVOR MILLS

Potential suicides

Most suicide risks are among ordinary people with no mental illness – ordinary, everyday people stricken with worry, dispirited by disaster, beaten down by their personal problems. To enumerate some of the misfortunes that can dispirit us: bereavement, loss of security, loss of job, redundancy, loss of social status; the failures: matrimonial failure, failure to get expected promotion, failure to pass examinations; and the *fear* of failure, because the students take their overdoses *before* the exams which they dread, *not* after them. Anxieties, nagging anxieties that can't be relieved, about one's health, about the health of one's loved ones, and – loneliness.

These life situations are situations in which the victim may feel a bit shamefaced, a bit to blame, so he doesn't want to advertise them to anyone he knows, certainly not to his family, nor to his doctor, nor his priest. He's bursting to get it off his chest, discuss it with somebody. But it must be somebody he doesn't know, whose confidentiality he can trust, and whom he need never see again if and when he gets through his trouble.

GEORGE DAY

Suicide – a Coroner's point of view

My legal training possibly makes me very doubtful of all statistics, and I am nowhere more doubtful than in statistics about suicide. In this country, so far as I know, these statistics are only obtainable from the verdicts from Coroners' courts, and I have no doubt that *the figures are too low*. Before a verdict of suicide can legally be returned, the Coroner is, or should be, completely satisfied beyond doubt that the person has committed suicide 'in law'. This means that one has got to examine something that is not very relevant from your point of view. What's the legal definition of suicide? It's very simple – that the person has killed himself, having had the specific intention of doing so. There is the further legal requirement that the Coroner should not return a verdict unless he is completely satisfied on the evidence before him that this is in fact what has happened. There was a case in the High Court last year where an appeal was made by the relatives of the deceased to quash the verdict of suicide; the High Court came to the conclusion that the verdict was wrong, on the basis that the Coroner had returned his verdict on the balance of probability rather than upon a certainty.

H. HOWITT

The majority of suicides are not mentally ill

Assessment of the suicidal episode requires careful consideration of the act itself and of the life situation in which the act took place: of the state of affairs to which the suicidal episode appeared, at that time, to be the answer. Usually the wrong answer. Many would say that it is always the wrong answer though one does from time to time find situations in which one has to admit that in all logic suicide just does make sense and in which one might oneself very well choose suicide; underlining a point which is often forgotten, that not every suicidal person is mentally ill. It is easy to assume that anyone who feels like ending it all must be *ipso facto* insane, but this is an immature view, reflecting personal anxieties about death, and not one which fits the facts. Clear evidence of psychotic disorder is only found in about one-third of cases of successful suicide, and of less significant mental instability in a further one-third, though these figures are often disputed.

RICHARD FOX

The human factor in suicide prevention

Most people who are interested in suicide prevention have heard of the sorry record which Berlin holds in respect of the *suicide rate*. West Berlin has a population of just under $2\frac{1}{4}$ million. About 900 people a year kill themselves there, i.e. two to three a day. This means that the suicide rate is over 40 per 100,000 of the population, more than twice what it is in the Federal Republic of Germany, and four times what it is in this country. At a fairly conservative estimate, the attempted suicides would be about 8,000 a year.

It seems, therefore, that this has to be accepted as more or less unchanging, and it was not accidental that the first service in Germany, similar to that of The Samaritans in this country and influenced by them and the ideas of their founder, was started in Berlin in 1956. The idea was to give to people in despair or tempted to suicide the possibility of seeing, if necessary immediately, someone who is able and willing to listen to and talk with such a client in distress at any time of the day, or to do so on the telephone at any time of the day or night.

Some of us in Germany very much admire the system of *befriending* as practised by The Samaritans in this country, because it provides practical and tangible proof of their concern and compassion for the client in distress and gives help which, I think, cannot be given in any other way.

ELLEN BALASZESKUL

Danger signs of acute suicide risk

1. Client withdrawn, cannot relate to you. Medical aid needed.
2. Family history of suicide.
3. Earlier attempts at suicide.
4. Definite idea how suicide would be committed. The tidying up of affairs indicate suicide is being planned.
5. Anxious tone to depressive picture.
6. Dependence on alcohol or drugs.
7. Some painful physical illness and long sleep disturbance.
8. Feeling of uselessness. In elderly, lack of acceptance of retirement.
9. Isolation, loneliness and uprooting.
10. The possibility of having to live with few human contacts.
11. Lack of a philosophy of life such as a comforting type of religious faith.
12. Financial worries.
13. Within the period of the rise and fall in mood, the most dangerous time is often when the client appears better. Now he has enough energy to kill himself.

The Samaritan contribution to suicide prevention*

Richard Fox

First, I want to try to show that 24-hour, publicised, anti-suicide services cut suicide rates and that the 34 per cent drop in suicide in England and Wales from 1963 to 1970 is associated with the growth of the largest suicide prevention organisation in the world. Secondly, I wish to describe some features of that organisation.

Suicide reduction

Looking first at the suicide drop, this would appear, from the international survey reported at the last International Association for Suicide Prevention conference in London to be unique, apart only from Japan (25·7 per cent in 1958 down to 14·7 per cent in 1965) where special cultural factors operated and war-torn Israel, where there was a drop from 12·1 per cent in 1962 to 9.9 per cent in 1966,[1] though I'm

* Revised and updated from an address to the 6th International Conference for Suicide Prevention, Mexico City, December 1971, and reprinted by kind permission of the International Association for Suicide Prevention and Prof. Robert E. Litman, Editor of the *Proceedings*.

told it has since risen. Elsewhere, the rates, where known, appear to have been static or to have gone up. In Australia in the 1960s they went up sharply and then dropped back.

TABLE I

	Population in millions England and Wales	Number of suicides England and Wales	Rate per 100,000 England and Wales	Samaritan Branches in UK on 31 Dec.	Number of new clients	Number of Volunteers
1959	43·39	5,207	11·5	2	Not recorded	Not recorded
1960	45·76	5,112	11·2	7	,, ,,	,, ,,
1961	46·17	5,200	11·3	17	,, ,,	,, ,,
1962	46·67	5,588	12·0	28	,, ,,	,, ,,
1963	47·02	5,714	12·2	41	,, ,,	,, ,,
1964	47·40	5,566	11·7	56	12,355	,, ,,
1965	47·76	5,161	10·8	68	16,422	6,537
1966	48·08	4,994	10·4	75	20,875	7,116
1967	48·39	4,711	9·7	86	31,780	7,688
1968	48·67	4,584	9·4	92	42,241	11,204
1969	48·83	4,370	8·9	95	51,412	8,910
1970	48·94	3,939	8·0	115	68,531	12,832
1971	48·81	3,945	8·08	122	89,254	15,225
1972*		3,819		132	156,722	15,729

Drop: 1963–71—34%

* Estimated first six months, 1939; first nine months, 2864

The impact on suicide rates of a suicide prevention service, controlled against areas without such a service, has been shown by Ringel in Vienna,[2] Plzak in Prague,[3] Litman and Farberow in Los Angeles,[4] Bill in Delaware[5], and Resnik in Florida.[6] The best study is that of Bagley,[7] who chose 15 towns in which The Samaritans had Branches operating at least two years prior to 1964, and 15 similar towns which at that time did not have a Branch. He calculated the average rates of suicide calculated for years operating, and for same number of years before The Samaritans started. He found that the average change in the 'Samaritan' towns was a reduction of 5·84 per cent, whilst the average change in suicide rate in 'Control' towns was an increase of 19·84 per cent. He has been criticised on the two samples and has repeated his calculations using two different 'Control' groups, but still finding a statistically significant difference.

Social factors – industrial crises, inflation and steeply rising unemployment – should, in theory, have sent suicide shooting up.[8] Can we attribute the drop to better medical treatment? I can think of no real advances in anti-depressive therapy during the last ten years and the psychiatric services in UK expanded very little for economic reasons. Electric shock treatment – the most rapid and effective of all treatments in suicidal depressions – has been available since the war without apparently affecting suicide rates anywhere. The introduction of non-poisonous domestic gas has been held to account for the drop in suicide but the objection to this is that decline in gas poisonings seems in many areas to have antedated the safer gas. It is highly doubtful how far people know whether their gas is safe or not (you can asphyxiate yourself with the new gas and some people have) and in Switzerland and Holland the new gas has led only to people turning to other methods, the suicide rate remaining the same. This change in the pattern of suicidal behaviour – which varies enormously from country to country – seems to be a question of fashion. The number of self-poisonings seem to have risen steeply through this time.[9] Intensive care units have increased in number and efficiency, so that many lives are now saved that would have been lost ten years ago. However, I have no evidence that our doctors are more cautious in prescribing or efficient in treating than their colleagues in comparable countries. The drop in suicide and rise in what is loosely called 'attempted suicide' underlines the observations of Stengel[10] that these are different, albeit overlapping, phenomena. The biggest single group of those engaging in non-fatal self-injury seem to be mostly young harassed housewives – not a numerous group among (fatal) suicides.

Why the numbers of overdose cases admitted to hospital should have shot up from an estimated 15,900 in 1957 to 50,400 in 1964 and possibly 90,000 in 1970[9] is a matter for speculation. Advertising pressure on doctors to prescribe an ever-increasing range of tranquillisers has doubtless been coupled with greater desire of people to seek relief from the minor degrees of distress which their parents apparently tolerated more stoically. One seems to be dealing with a national epidemic, a sort of socially contagious disorder. One's observation of several hundred of such patients each year, after recovery, is that they show predominantly the often described 'cry for help', they want to manipulate some life situation, or else simply the desire for a period of oblivion. Only about 15 per cent appear to regret having been resuscitated. I do not personally believe that this epidemic augurs the imminent breakdown of civilisation Professor Ivor Mills has suggested, but it does present The Samaritans with perhaps their biggest challenge.

Every large town now has a branch of The Samaritans and, sparsely populated rural areas in Wales and Scotland apart, there is virtually nationwide coverage, 127 of the 138 branches being on a 24-hour alert.* These vary from London, with a suite of rooms, two whole-time Deputy Directors, 400 volunteers and some 10,000 new clients per year; down to small country branches seeing maybe a dozen old clients, and a few new ones, per week. Postal services

* At time of going to press.

using a box number exist in rural areas of Yorkshire and the Scottish Highlands. A national organisation enforces uniformity of standards in selection, training, branch procedure and, now, advertising. In 1971, a Branch was closed down for failing to meet the required standard.

There is a Director or Chairman, Leaders who share in the administration, training, and supervision and who carry out 'diagnostic' interviews, and sometimes, counselling. The volunteers, who average 110 per branch, man the telephone, interview clients and carry out 'befriending', which is simply the offering of friendship by one ordinary human being to another at a time of crisis or loneliness, but subject to leadership supervision. The befriending, and *advertised* immediate 24-hour availability are the special features of the service. Other organisations run 24-hour services but do not, in UK anyhow, *ask* to be rung up in the middle of the night by people who feel miserable. Yet the reactively depressed who worsen with the night and the endogenously depressed who feel worst when they wake early, need help most urgently at these times.

The volunteers

Applicants are interviewed and subjected to a standardised process of selection and preparation training, comprising seven lecture discussions, telephone answering in a mock-up situation, supervised telephone duty and ongoing case conferences. The drop out/reject rate varies from the 93 of 100 consecutive applicants who went during one period last year to the London Branch to a national average of probably 60 per cent, and standards for selection are rising. The Maudsley Personality Inventory profile of 200 volunteers from Eastern branches showed them to be less neurotic than average and slightly more extroverted. The best Leaders were extroverts, the best telephone answerers introvert and the best befrienders stable introverts. Those scoring low or zero on neuroticism tended either to be liars or so insensitive to the emotional needs of others that they were unsuitable.[11]

Volunteers come from all walks of life with the inevitable middle-class preponderance. They include mental health professionals at all levels, though the change of role involved in befriending often makes these doubtful quantities as volunteers. Mostly they act as branch consultants: almost all branches have a psychiatric consultant and work closely with the area psychiatric service though The Samaritans remain emphatically *outside* the statutory service. The movement remains an essentially lay organisation although we know of 300 to 400 doctors active in the work (five have been branch directors). The 'unofficial' nature of The Samaritans attracts many clients who are unwilling for one of many reasons to go to an 'official' source for help.

An interesting off-shoot of The Samaritans has been 'Nightline' services in universities manned by students, of which about half a dozen in the UK are currently running. These meet a real need in a suicide-prone group which is under-represented among Samaritan clients.[12]

The clients

These have been studied on a nationwide basis in 1966 when 12,355 report forms were computer analysed and, more comprehensively, in 1969 when the number was 35,276. The data would fill several books but some findings of interest are that the clients resemble the general population in sex/age structure apart from a considerable deficiency of the suicide-prone over-sixties – 8 per cent of all clients in 1966 and 6 per cent in 1969. Under 25s amounted to 16 per cent though many branches have recorded a more recent spurt of young clients. Inter-branch variation is considerable and not always explicable demographically: thus in 1969 one client in fifteen was aged 15–24 in Blackpool compared with one in four in Havering (East London); and for over-65s the variation was even greater: from 1:115 in the big London branch to 1:5 in Bexhill.

The social class spread was also even with 14 per cent 'professional or executive', 31 per cent 'unskilled' and the remainder evenly divided between 'clerical', 'skilled' and 'semi-skilled'. A disproportionate 21 per cent were unemployed, far above the national figures for 1969; but there was no seasonal fluctuation other than the usual spring and autumn bulges which apply to all categories analysed. If the unemployment were the cause of referral, the figures should have dropped in spring and summer, but they did not. October was the busiest month in 1966 and 1969 – the excess over spring being accounted for by the steadily rising case load. When client numbers stabilise, it will be possible to see whether the suicide and client referral rates run as parallel as they seem to now.

There is the usual excess of single (28 per cent), separated (8 per cent), divorced (4 per cent), and widowed (7 per cent). Again, these groups were distributed through the year as above. People contacting The Samaritans at night were high-risk cases judged by previous suicidal behaviour. About 8 per cent rang between midnight and 8 a.m. in both years but in 1969 we know that only 7 per cent rang who had no suicidal history against 9 per cent for 'prior attempt', 11 per cent for 'many attempts' and 13 per cent for 'attempt now'. There was a total of 753 of the latter during 1969. About 33 per cent of our clients called or rang between 18.00 and midnight with the day's peak (2,650) from 20.00–21.00. There was no peak as the public houses closed. Calls dropped to 704 from 24.00–01.00 then rose to 1,824 and 1,102 each for the next two hours, dropping steeply to a trough of 102 from 06.00–07.00 and then rising to a midday sub-peak. The evening hours also showed an excess of previously suicidal cases. The 'attempts now' peak was 01.00–02.00 when 1 in 30 people ringing had attempted suicide. The average was 1 in 56.

The problems brought by clients were assessed in 1969 under forty categories, the largest being 'marital difficulties' (12 per cent). 'Loneliness', 'depression', 'worry over third party', 'anxiety/obsessions', 'inadequate personality', and 'household debt' were large groups, but as data go, these are pretty soft. 'Crime committed' and 'acute mental illness' were each recorded in just under 1 per cent. Again, distribution through the year was as above.

The Samaritan clients who lapse are a suicide-prone group with a rate during the year after lapsing of 30 to 40 times the national average.[13] Before 1972 there was officially no follow-up, leaving it to the client to contact The Samaritans or not as he wished but this is changing as we try to make Leaders more aware of high-risk cases. Quite a few clients later become volunteers – perhaps amounting to 10 per cent of volunteers nationally.

Publicity of many kinds has established The Samaritans as a national institution: it even has Royal patronage and is in grave danger of becoming respectable. A weekly series of 11 television programmes, *The Befrienders*, portrayed the work of a Samaritan branch in fictional form. Even before this series, three surveys had shown that two-thirds of the population at large knew about The Samaritan organisation and what it did, and of these, two-thirds would be willing to seek its help if they needed it. This may account for The Samaritans' effectiveness in preventing suicide compared with, notably, America where there are some 300 Suicide Prevention Centres but no kind of coherent national organisation or image. The apparent ineffectiveness of emergency telephone services on the continent of Europe, also, may be accounted for by their relatively small numbers and intimate link, in some countries, with evangelical churches. The preventative effect of Samaritan work has been questioned on the grounds that doctors see so many more suicidal people and Barraclough[14] found in parts of Southern England that only 4 per cent of suicides had been to Samaritans against over 80 per cent who had been to doctors. Maybe, however, effective suicide prevention here is similar to effective police work which is measured by crimes prevented rather than by those cleared up. All branches meet clients who have carried a newspaper clipping with local branch details in their wallets maybe for years before making a call.

Conclusions

The 'social model' of suicide advocated by Durkheim[15] seems to be suggested while the 'medical model' does not. The Samaritans appear to have reduced suicide by altering society. The movement has of course long been non-religious and non-evangelistic: Belfast continues to recruit volunteers from Protestants, Catholics and others, proportionate to the general population, and religious or communal conflicts have never arisen in branches. However, when I first wrote about The Samaritans in 1962[16] I said that the (then small) organisation 'could represent a tremendous resurgence of practical Christianity'. It seems to have been just that. It seems also to have shown itself a most effective and, I believe, almost the only statistically proven agency working in preventive psychiatry.

References

1. FOX, R. (Ed.), *Proceedings of Fifth International Conference for Suicide Prevention*, London 1969. IASP 1970, pp. 6–35.

2. RINGEL, E., *op. cit.*, Ref. 1, p. 13.

3. PLZAK, M., Personal communication. The Prague rate dropped 15 per cent in the first year compared with a continuing upward trend in other large towns.

4. LITMAN, R. E. AND FARBEROW, N. L., *op. cit.*, Ref. 1, pp. 246–50.

5. BILL, A. Z., *op. cit.*, Ref. 1, pp. 239–42.

6. RESNIK, H. L. P., *Current Psych. Therapies*, 1964, IV, 253.

7. BAGLEY, C., *Soc. Sci. & Med.*, 1968, **2**, 1.

8. HENRY, A. F. AND SHORT, J. F., *Suicide and Homicide, New York, 1964*.

9. MILLS, I., Paper to Samaritan National Conference, Sept. 1971.

10. STENGEL, E. AND COOK, N. G., *Attempted Suicide*, OUP, 1958.

11. DAY, G., Norwich Samaritans. Research in progress.

12. FOX, R., *Roy. Soc. Hlth. J.*, 1971, 91:4, 180–5.

13. BARRACLOUGH, B. M., *Lancet*, 1970, **2**, 868.

14. BARRACLOUGH, B. M., *Brit. J. Psychiat*, 1972.

15. DURKHEIM, E., *Le Suicide*, Paris, 1897.

16. FOX, R., *Lancet*, 1962, **2**, 1102–5.

The management of the suicidal patient – a psychiatrist's view*

Richard Fox

The great majority of suicidal acts are not fatal. The majority of these, probably, are not entirely meant to be, and many are not meant to be at all. Feelings towards life and death are characteristically mixed, the one tending to dominate the other. To comprehend adequately the suicidal act, one must take into account the extent to which the person has 'risked' his life in the proceeding. The person who takes four aspirin and calls the doctor probably doesn't mean very seriously to die, but even here appearances can be misleading. It could represent an impulsive attempt in an ignorant person who immediately regretted the act. The next impulse might be to jump in front of a moving train. The overdose – 96 per cent of 456 cases admitted to 5 UK hospitals in 1972 – allows the possibility firstly of a change of mind and, secondly, of the chance that you will be discovered in time. It is a gamble, as it were, with life and death. In the assessment of the suicidal person, the method has to be carefully inquired into. The more the person has planned and thought the thing out

* From a talk given at The Samaritans' National Conference, 1965.

the more serious it all becomes. Shooting, jumping and hanging are of more serious import than overdose, especially with aspirin, or gassing.

One sometimes comes across the person – the uncommon, true 'endogenous' depressive, who appears, for no apparent real reason, to have become steadily more and more miserable, apathetic, disinterested in life and work, coping less and less well with both, irritable, sleepless, with poor appetite, taking pleasure from nothing – who will try to end his state of general misery. Such a person is likely to have had relations who have had depressive illnesses and, maybe, have ended their lives. He will be more likely to have a special solid type of body build and to be of cyclothymic, i.e. 'up and down' temperament, and there are measurable changes in brain biochemistry. Much more usually, in cases of depression, one finds a recent story of social adversity – jobs lost, love affairs broken, relations dead, bankruptcy threatened, kids in trouble, husband absconded with the lady next door – and, of course, the very special threats of physical disease and of the physiological crises: puberty, menstruation, childbirth, menopause. Most usually one finds a number of factors combined together, any of which in themselves would be weathered without distress, but which in their cumulative effect prove to be overwhelming. We all have our breaking points, and they are different.

Doctors usually divide depressive illness into 'endogenous' and 'reactive' groups, but there is much overlapping and a few doubt the validity of these 'pigeon holes' at all. Certainly 'pure' cases are few, but the classification helps if it makes the doctor analyse as carefully as he can the background to the disorder.

So, a suicidal act is an indication of crisis, which, if properly understood and dealt with insightfully, can lead to a positive and constructive outcome. Washing the stomach out in Casualty and sending the patient straight home is seldom much help. It is not necessary to have everyone in hospital, especially in a psychiatric hospital, but admission somewhere is a good general rule. It underlines the seriousness of what has taken place, it separates people who have been in conflict, it allows tensions and crises to resolve. It allows someone outside the family, whether it is the house physician, the social worker, the Samaritan visitor, the hospital chaplain or the psychiatrist (better not all five at once doing different things) to find out what has been going on and help towards a constructive solution. A crisis is a good thing so long as you learn from it, so that even a suicidal attempt can be 'good' provided useful things flow from it. Plenty of situations crawl along in chronic misery for years when a good-going suicidal attempt at the beginning might have made somebody 'do something' and have been very useful. But there are other ways, and better ways.

The psychiatric management of the suicidal patient depends upon as precise a formulation of the problem as can be achieved, leading usually to removal of the patient to a place of safety, whether the medical ward of a nearby hospital or some kind of psychiatric unit for observation and treatment. Very occasionally, the removal is carried out under a Compulsory Order. One always hates doing this, but doctors are less worried than some imagine about the effects on the patient of removal, perhaps struggling, by three or four policemen, two ambulance men and the social worker. Though one has ordered this on a good number of occasions with psychotic patients of all types, one has yet to meet anyone who, on recovery, showed animosity. But one has met gratitude, and the comment: 'Why didn't somebody do something before?' The recovered patient realises often better than other people just how uncontrollable things are at rock bottom, and he may indeed come to you, saying 'Doctor, I don't feel safe, I don't feel in control, please take me into your hospital and protect me from myself'. It is right that The Samaritans should eschew compulsory methods because I think it is good to have a nationwide service that just never acts against a client's wishes, whether to hand a murderer to the police or a psychotic to a doctor. But one hopes they will not feel too badly about doctors or the police using Orders sometimes, nor feel guilty should they find themselves, if obliquely, associated somehow with some form of Order. The doctor's duty is to his patient and to his patient's best interest – which may include restricting him while temporarily not responsible for his actions. To act otherwise would be irresponsible and lay one open to criticism and even prosecution. My hospital, with about 1,000 patients, has about 2,500 admissions per year, of which roughly 1 in 10 comes under some kind of Compulsory Order, and this is typical of the country as a whole.

The Samaritan faced with a truly desperate patient will, of course, not conduct the type of interrogation outlined. He will certainly not stop the client from talking if the client wants to get some pressing anxiety out of his system, but that is a different matter. Eliciting the relevant facts from a suicidal patient is essentially psychiatric history taking, and is what doctors and social workers have been trained over years to do. Samaritans are not pretending to be psychiatrists or social workers, and are not going to ask the client out of the blue whether he has been hearing voices, or seducing the neighbour's wife. You may or may not tell your best friends about your secret anxieties, but you don't expect them to prise them from you willy-nilly, and the Samaritan is expecting to become the client's friend. Friendship is what he is offering, not diagnosis and treatment. The psychiatrist is not offering patients this kind of friendship, and gently avoids it when they attempt to get on social terms with him by inviting him out to supper or whatever. So any interrogation is done by an experienced person such as the director or left to the doctor. The Samaritan can best be compared with the first aid worker called to the scene of a road accident. He does not set broken limbs, open the abdomen, put up blood transfusions. The most he would venture to do would be to bind up the patient's wounds as best he could, and send him along to the nearest surgeon to be treated properly, but he might simply protect the patient from interference or disturbance, whilst holding his hand, and making reassuring noises.

If the client is in a desperate way, the Samaritan is likely to lead the conversation round to the possibility of medical treatment. The client is likely to have a variety of misconceptions about the local mental hospital, gathered from local folklore over generations when the place was a good deal grimmer than it is now. Relations between the Samaritan Branch and its area mental hospital should be close. This means not only that the psychiatric consultant should be a senior man from that hospital, but that he should be seen to be an active consultant to the branch, drawn into the instruction of volunteers, referring lonely patients of his for befriending, attendant at occasional case conferences (or whatever you like to call them) and generally wanted and useful. Do something in return if you can, show some interest in his hospital and the activities attached to it – have a representative on the League of Friends, get some volunteers to carry the tins around for Mental Health Flag Day. Above all, don't be too frightened to visit the place. Most mental hospitals have Open Days. Go and see where your clients will be admitted when they get suicidal, so that you can re-assure them from the basis of personal knowledge. Electric shock treatment (ECT) is often a special worry, but the way it is done now with a general anaesthetic makes it less alarming than having a tooth out. Patients even ask for 'some more of that nice treatment'.

People who obviously need to come into hospital may be frightened to take the step. It does happen rarely that a client, suicidal and yet refusing medical attention, has to be sat with by Samaritans for many hours in relays until the suicidal phase passes or he changes his mind about seeing a doctor. The really suicidal patient must not be left alone. The Samaritan need not be too alarmed at undertaking what is really a piece of psychiatric nursing, because it is almost unheard of for a suicidal patient to attack an attendant. Suicidal people are very seldom violent to others, and when they are, they attack those most beloved to them, having projected upon them in a delusional way the grief and hopelessness which they feel themselves.

There is another important reason why the liaison between the psychiatric hospital and the Samaritan Branch should be close. The hospital, whether Samaritans like it or not, sees many times more really desperate people than the Samaritan Branch does. Though this has changed in recent years in some branches a really suicidal client is comparatively rare, yet they run an elaborate rota, 24-hour manning, premises in the middle of the town, and a lot of useful activities connected with the branch. This can become a sledge hammer to crack a nut. Active volunteers have been known to go months, and even years, without seeing a suicidal person. The question of how much money and effort the saving of a single life deserves is a moot ethical question: the point is that Samaritain services in many parts of the country are under-used. In contrast to this, the hospital services are being over-used. Probably no hospital can claim to be coping *really* adequately with the suicidal patients who come to it. But working together, the hospital service and the Samaritans, referring people to each other freely, always with their consent of course, can do much better. We know that the suicidal attempt is a repetitive phenomenon. Someone who has attempted his life is at risk of attempting it again. Ten per cent will eventually succeed. The doctor, with the hospital services at his disposal, is usually better than The Samaritans at dealing with the suicidal crisis. Let us just note, however, that there are by now many Samaritans with far more practical experience of the suicidal than most professionals! Samaritans are probably better than the doctor at preventing some suicidal episodes from recurring. This prevention may be less exciting, less sensational, and apparently less immediately rewarding. But in the long term, it is far more important.

Arising from inadequate use of Samaritan services is the problem of suicide in the elderly. The Samaritan organisation has long recorded statistics, and one thing that emerged from the earliest studies of Samaritan clients was that their age-graph does not coincide with the age-graph of suicides. Thus, the suicide figures rise with increasing age. Over the age of 60, on the other hand, Samaritan clients become fewer and fewer. Thought still needs to be given to ways in which this class of potential or actual suicidal person can be brought to the help they need. New thinking and new techniques are required here. No one regards the present Samaritan organisation as the best of all possible organisations, and some may want to try, or may already be trying, new approaches to this aspect of suicide prevention. It may be necessary for Samaritans to go out from behind their telephones and find the clients that don't ring them up. Certainly there is a need for *every* branch to make its work known to all the professional groups – GPs, district nurses, health visitors, social workers of all kinds – who know where the hidden lonely and suicide-prone people are. The rule against third-party referral does not apply to those by professionals, or of the elderly.

There is a category of mild or transiently suicidal person who is managed perfectly well by Samaritans without the help of the medical authorities at any stage, like the acutely depressed, desperate or dispirited person, reacting to some very real catastrophe, a bereavement, a broken love affair, being sacked. Life suddenly seems to lose all meaning, the person cries all night, and feels much better in the morning. Many recover without anyone knowing, others are supported by their families or the family doctor. This group of psychiatric conditions is less clearly understood and described than the more catastrophic depressive reactions, and some of the more sophisticated Samaritan branches probably have unique experience with it. Not all, obviously: one of the mistakes a Samaritan branch may make in the early stages is to assume that goodwill, energy and God's guidance are everything, whereas in fact it takes a great deal of diligence and discipline to do this job properly, whether as a branch or as an individual.

Given this willingness to study and learn, the Samaritan 'amateur' need feel at no disadvantage to the medical or social work 'professional'. The trained and experienced Samaritan has as much claim to a place in the relief of human distress as anyone else.

Helping people in anxiety

H. J. Walton

A person in adulthood feels 'good' to the extent that his relations with his parents were satisfactory. A person who had bad relations with a parent will be prone, throughout life, to experience spells of 'bad' feelings: self-criticism, inferiority, depression or anxiety. In this sense the exact nature of a person's associations with his parents remain embedded in him and are a source of feeling states which can occur to him throughout adulthood.

The people we see in crisis, therefore, talk to us about their present social relationships, their own family members, and at length also about relationships they had with their parents.

A person communicates with other people by means of speech. He communicates with himself by thinking. Thought is internal behaviour. In an interview we enable the person we are helping to give us access to his internal behaviour, by asking him to tell us about his thoughts.

In our attempt to understand behaviour through talking to a person, a double task faces us. We have to understand the person in the first place, and then we have to comprehend the situation in which he finds himself. When his crisis is the result of external difficulties or pressures, we can talk of *press*, as when someone loses an important person through death. When the crisis is the result of internal pressures inside the troubled individual, we can speak of *stress*. Such internal stress can be produced by thoughts in a person's mind, by feelings such as anger or resentment, or by impulses such as sexual urges which trouble the person but which he cannot allow full expression.

A useful way of looking at people in crisis may be by assuming that when they contact us they are disturbed by painful inner tension: they suffer from anxiety which has reached an insupportable level. Anxiety is caused by the human environment. It is a mood of fear which puts out of action a whole range of normal skills and functions. An anxious person does not attend adequately to his environment, does not notice things, makes errors, is forgetful. Generally, anxiety serves to disorganise ordinary behaviour.

Anxiety can increase in intensity to produce a state of terror. If a person is appropriately predisposed, there is a wide range of life events which can precipitate a state of anxiety.

Being rejected by another person is one: as when an employee is told that his work is not good enough, or a husband tells his wife that her housekeeping does not satisfy his expectations. (Perhaps his standards are over-conscientious, ingrained in him by an excessively perfectionist mother when he was young.)

The other person may precipitate anxiety in our client or patient by more clear-cut aggression or hostility, making threats which endanger the security of the person who consults us. It can be, however, that there is no other person prominently implicated; instead it may be a person's own thoughts which precipitate anxiety in him: a mother suffering from fearfulness that she is not good enough to care for her child and will inadvertently perpetrate some harmful or even fatal accident. Thoughts connected with sex are often extremely distressing to people, and if we get from them details about their past lives, it is clear how the conflict state about sex arose. They need to express their responses of loving and physical tenderness, but there are forbidding images or memories lodged in their minds which forbid such natural expressions of love.

We arrive at mature forms of sexuality only in adulthood, passing through phases which society considers abnormal, indeed will not recognise as customary or common at certain stages of life. We forget the devious paths by which adolescents arrive at mature sexuality.

The person who contacts us will usually be in a state of excessive anxiety. This is a painful inner state, a pervasive sensation of fear which is uncomfortable and in extreme cases may be intolerable. Anxiety is so distressing a state that, when it is severe, the sufferer will seek to reduce the painful tension, sometimes in ways which lead him to suffer great harm.

There are various kinds of anxiety, with three main types. The importance of distinguishing the type of anxiety lies in the fact that for each type a different kind of approach is required.

A person may have extreme, massive anxiety because he fears he will be suddenly isolated, or because he is suddenly overwhelmed with self-reproach or self-loathing, or because he dreads that some harm is about to befall him in relation to his body.

The first type of anxiety, the dread of isolation, occurs when a person is suddenly deprived of the support of another person upon whom he had been more deeply dependent than perhaps he knew. He may lose the protecting person through death; a woman may lose the husband on whom she is emotionally dependent because he leaves her for another woman; a person may never have married in order to retain the protectiveness of a parent, and be precipitated into an anxiety attack if the parent withdraws affection or support.

This type of separation anxiety has been studied in small children who are taken from parents when admitted to hospital; but you can also see very similar reactions in adults, say in a woman whose husband leaves on a business trip overseas, or in someone whose more emotionally robust marriage partner becomes ill.

The second type of anxiety, the anxiety of self-disgust, is different. Healthy people have a reasonable appreciation of their own attainments; they tell themselves that, considering the obstacles they have encountered, they have acquitted themselves fairly adequately. But the anxiety which comes from an unhealthy conscience leads a person to think that he has failed, that he betrayed all the trust reposed in him, that he is a disgrace to those who had believed in him. This type of anxiety leads the person to say to whoever is approached for help: 'Please don't let my mother or father hear of this.' Such a person will figuratively beat his head, overcome with self-hatred and abnegation. They may say that they deserve only condemnation or punishment. Some may actually punish themselves, taking their chastisement in their own hands. These people are flayed by their consciences. Psychologically they have, as part of their minds, attitudes of self-disgust. These attitudes are seen by psychiatrists as stemming from hatred or criticism or rejection experienced during growing up. Disliked by a parent, they have come to carry for ever, as part of their mentality, the inner reflection of what was once directed upon them from the censorious parent. Now it has become a part of the self. Any criticism they evoke, a failure of their efforts, or even a reproof uttered by someone in the heat of anger, suddenly lights up their own stores of self-criticism.

Only someone who has experienced the horror of being alone in a state of terror while the full light of consciousness plays relentlessly over all the weakness, failures, omissions and faults, can understand the fear which may be felt by somebody who regards himself as beyond contempt. Often such a person, when seeking help, is in an extreme dread that he has failed, that he is an outcast and will be despised if only people knew.

We recognise that when a person seeks our help for anxiety of this self-despising variety we will probably find in his life history a parent who was not able to feel appropriate affection for him. This parent is then retained in his mind throughout life as a sort of inner assailant, who can undermine him, bring him down, humiliate him. His precarious self-esteem drops to an agitatingly low level when in addition he encounters criticism or rejection in his current experience with other people.

The third type of anxiety, dread of physical damage, may be illustrated by its expression in a young man: 'Lately I go to bed many nights haunted by the fear that I won't wake up the following morning. I can assure you this fear of dying is torture to go through.'

The person is suddenly struck with terrible certainty by a fear that his heart is diseased, or that he has a cancer. People anxious in this way, overcome by a fear of some serious physical affliction, are likely to seek medical reassurance directly, so they are more prone to have their first recourse to doctors than to any other sort of helping person.

To give first aid to people with these varying types of anxiety calls for very different responses in the helping person. The individual with separation anxiety needs substitute company from a friend or a relative, or hospital care. The person with conscience anxiety, convinced of his worthlessness, needs a personal response which will revive his self-esteem. To protect and provide comfort and care for him, as advocated for the earlier type of separation anxiety, may only convince him of his worthlessness. The person with the third type of anxiety, fear of bodily dissolution, usually needs medical attention as a first step, before tracing out with him what the roots of his physical panic were.

While we may approve of the wisdom of those in trouble who seek help, they themselves may consider their help-seeking despicable. Jerome Frank has demonstrated that one of the changes occurring in people who are successfully treated by psychiatrists is their greater effectiveness in getting help for themselves when they feel troubled. Some people approaching us will show, as part of their personality disturbance which has not yet been improved by treatment, a great hesitancy in asking for help. Many of our clients or patients will reach us only when the extremity of their distress has pushed them over this inner barrier against asking for aid. They will often be ashamed and apologetic at this weakness, as they see it, this lapse into open admission of lack of independence. Many will not come to see us until their distress has driven them to contemplate suicide.

*   *   *

Anxiety

Neurosis is a state in which unconscious drives and fears are at war with conscious ones, causing a conflict which the victim can't resolve. Everyone is, to a lesser or greater extent, neurotic, and thank God for it, for without neurosis we would have no poets, no artists, no composers, no eccentrics. We should lose our rich world of fantasy and imagination. So, one might ask, at what point does neurosis require treatment? And I would say 'when it get to the stage of crippling a person's life, and handicapping the lives of those around him'.

Anxiety may be given two broad classifications – floating and specific. Floating anxiety will find a way to attach itself to absolutely anything past, present or future. It is a never-ending round of fear, uncertainty, indecision, guilt and remorse. It wears out the sufferer and everyone around him. It begins as he wakes, follows him through the day and often bedevils him in dreams at night. It has been recognised as a very real illness and needs medical treatment. You will detect it because your client will bring a multitude of symptoms and a catalogue of causes. The causes will vary tremendously in importance, but the severity of anxiety attached to them remains the same. Thus a woman will worry as much about her children's safety and her husband's health as she will over the cooking of a casserole and the cleaning of her floor. And as soon as she is reassured on one point she will move to another.

Specific anxiety gives you much more scope. Your clients will attach this to something which has happened or which they fear will happen, to a set of circumstances, to a change in their lives, to a long-standing characteristic threatening to overwhelm them. They will not necessarily be people always prone to anxiety. Their great need will be to talk to someone who will neither criticise nor judge nor advise, but who will listen, perhaps at great length, warmly, attentively and with compassion. As they talk, they will clarify the issue. The need to find precise words will pin-point their feelings, will help to get the anxiety into perspective. The chance to confide without interruption will release the tension and the pain will become more tolerable. They may feel ashamed of their fears and reluctant to go into detail. Having already bored and exasperated their family and friends they will find immense relief in your interest and total acceptance. You may find they need professional expert advice, medical, legal, financial, and you must know to whom they should be referred. But always your role will be to help them shoulder the burden. You are not expected to remove it.

Inadequate personalites bordering on the psychopathic are often on our doorstep. They seem to have no sense of what is generally known as 'right or wrong'; no 'conscience'; no feelings of responsibility; no forethought. They flout the accepted rules of behaviour in this country in the twentieth century, and because they cannot submit to authority, they are always in trouble. They change jobs rapidly; are often unemployed. They marry, have children, and abandon their families. They commit petty crimes, the penalties for which far outweigh the rewards. They are impulsive, impetuous, unrealistic, unreliable, untruthful and often full of charm. By the time they get to us, they have usually gone through most of the mills. You will probably find them pleasant to befriend. They talk easily, they are grateful for the attention they get. They will encourage you to feel you are helping them greatly. You will be correspondingly elated and subsequently let down. Sadly, there is very little we can do for them.

MOLLY KEELAN

Anxiety of the volunteers

Samaritans tend to be conscientious, anxiety-prone people. We want to help, and our eagerness may defeat our object. Most of us have to learn how to listen, and what is more, how to cope with our own anxieties and the impatience which this exercise raises. We know that befriending is the most important thing we have to offer our clients, and we have to keep reminding ourselves that the greater part of befriending is expressed in listening. Unfortunately, we may be keen to keep it all on the very positive level, and be optimistic, so that we will want to encourage the client that it will work out all right, and that in no time he will feel on top of the world. Now it is fair enough to take a positive approach, but remember the client sets the pace: if you try to rush him into an optimistic frame of mind when he is not ready for it, the result will be that he feels you are expecting him to become optimistic, and whether he feels it or not he will try to be optimistic in order to please you. He may give you the impression he feels better and later you will read of his suicide.

There are very real dangers for religious volunteers. They may suffer from anxiety because they feel the need to protect Christ from criticism or lack of reverence, and therefore a need to evangelise, to enclose men and women within Catholic or Protestant churches. This creates a real risk of the misuse of power: those who seek our aid in a crisis are in a sensitive condition – they come with open emotional and spiritual wounds – and are ready candidates for manipulation and brain-washing.

One of the most vicious aspects of some religion today is the way its adherents seek to pass on their own faith second-hand to a person in trouble. Since it is not his own, it is certain to distort his personality and let him down in times of crisis. It is only a faith that an individual develops for himself that will lead to any degree of health, maturity or salvation. The Samaritan theological approach is to share the Passion of Christ and by suffering with the distressed person, establish the presence (not defined in words) of the crucified, loving Lord in that person's hell. Before the Church can share in being Transfigured there must be a share in being Disfigured. Saying 'Yes' to the challenge to follow the crucified Christ will mean saying 'No' to the temptation to believe that volunteers can only help the clients if they can persuade them to say they accept the religion of the helpers.

JOHN ELDRID

Befriending the sexually frustrated

Chad Varah

The Samaritans try not merely to keep people alive but to give them a reason to be glad to be alive. We shall not do that if we feel anything but the deepest compassion for their frustrations and deprivations and unsatisfied needs.

Amongst these needs is the need for sexual gratification. This is a need which we take most seriously but which the general public – both those who look down on it and those who flaunt it – seem to consider something dirty, and certainly something to be ashamed of in a person who is not regarded as young and attractive. The sexual appetite differs from appetites like hunger and thirst in one very important way: it does not kill you directly if it is not satisfied (it may kill you indirectly). The body cannot for unlimited periods do without food or drink or sleep, but sex is an appetite which can be left unsatisfied for interminable periods without causing the death of the body. If death supervenes it is because the effect upon the mind has been such as to make the person feel that life is not worth living, and therefore he destroys himself.

Where people have voluntarily chosen the way of celibacy,

which is a perfectly legitimate thing to do if you think God has called you to that, it is a medical fact that, although the organs tend to atrophy a little after a long time, no harm comes to the general health. It is not dangerous to the health to leave this particular appetite unsatisfied, speaking of it simply as a physical appetite and speaking of the general health of the body. Whatever conflicts or struggles the person may have if he has voluntraily chosen the way of re-direction are his own business. What we must never do, of course, is to recommend this way to somebody who already has a sufficiently heavy burden to carry without our stupid unthinking words being added to it. Never in The Samaritans do we say to somebody who is frustrated, 'Oh, you should sublimate'. Apart from the fact that this is a misuse of a technical term, what is meant is something easier said than done. One can only admire the way in which so many people who are undernourished in their sexual life somehow convert the energy which is not employed in personal sexual relationships into great benefits for large numbers of people – almost as though they were sharing their love amongst many people instead of devoting it to one person.

If someone mentions this unsatisfied need and there is nothing that we can do about it, we can at least refrain from implying that he ought not to have it, or ought not to talk about it, or ought not to grumble about it. We can agree that this is a painful experience, and we can sympathise. You might think it is not much help just to say, 'Yes, that is tough ... Yes, indeed, I do agree that is very hard.' Well, it may not be *much* help, but a little is better than nothing, and many of our clients have been somewhat comforted by the recognition that the cross they bear is heavy. At least they retire from the encounter with us with a certain amount of dignity instead of going away with the impression that we think they are making a great fuss about some quite small thing which it is perhaps sinful of them to experience in the first place. They go away feeling that their problem has been treated with the seriousness that it deserves and that they themselves have been recognised as people who quietly and unsung have been battling heroically in a very difficult field.

Sex is something which God has implanted in us – a need which serves a good many ends, one obvious one being the continuation of the species. Our bodies do not know this. Hardly ever does it happen that a man pays ardent court to a woman because he is determined to reproduce his species. I have never yet met a married man (this may only be because I do not know anybody who is a nineteenth baronet longing for an heir to be the twentieth) whose uppermost thought as he contemplated the privileges which go with Holy Matrimony was 'Now I can reproduce the species'. You do of course sometimes get people who, having married because they loved one another, have not been blessed with children, and seek professional advice about anything that may be preventing them from having any. That is a different matter. They did not court and marry one another in the first place in order to reproduce the species. They were simply diddled by Nature, which wants to reproduce the species, into doing so by gratifying appetites which Nature (Christians would say God) had implanted in them.

There are some people who talk as though to take pleasure in the gratification of the appetite of sex were somehow reprehensible. It would be blasphemous not to take pleasure in it, where God has devised something so admirable, so delightful. The enjoyable is meant to be enjoyed, and if someone doesn't enjoy that which is considered by discriminating people to be enjoyable, that is a sign not of great holiness in them but of some defect, like that of the person who cannot enjoy the music of Bach because he is tone deaf or lacking in cultural education or has poor taste or is simply incapable of really listening. It is a mistake if you are a human being to try to live as though you were merely an animal; it is a mistake to forget that you are an animal; it is a mistake to try to live as if you were an angel: it is a mistake to forget that there is something angelic or divine within each one, including the ones you might consider least likely. So the person who is suffering from lack of bread, or lack of water, or lack of sleep, should find his fellows giving these needs priority, for he not only suffers physically but also becomes obsessed with his need and is incapable of concentrating on other matters which they might consider 'prior' things.

There are certain things which are regarded by all cultivated persons everywhere as deeply enjoyable, and sexual experience, sexual gratification, is quite undeniably one of these. Therefore we are led into some useful practices such as the continuation of the race within reasonable bounds, building our nests, bringing up our families and so forth, by this provision of something which we, to a greater or lesser extent, ardently desire.

I say to a greater or lesser extent because the amount of sexual drive, the strength of this appetite or hunger, varies very considerably from individual to individual and even in the same individual from time to time. It tends to diminish with increasing age, I am sorry to have to tell you, and it also usually diminishes at times of being run down or ill: it is usually almost extinguished in times of severe depression. But however much it may vary from person to person or from time to time there is no normal human individual in whom it is completely lacking. It takes different forms in the male and in the female; the male being generally speaking more spontaneously sexed and the female more responsively sexed. One of the things which we frequently have to do in helping our clients is to interpret the opposite sex to them because so many men blame their womenfolk, not for being unwomanly, but for being womanly, for being the way women are, the way God made women. Similarly women blame men sometimes for being men. If you expect a woman to be the same kind of person sexually as a man but just with a differently shaped body, then you are expecting something which rarely happens. And if as a woman you are expecting a man to be like a woman apart from being furnished with a penis, again you are expecting something rarely encountered.

Men and women differ from one another in their fundamental attitude to sex, in the spontaneity of their physical urges, and in their general emotional make-up, as much as they do in their physical organs. Yet the difference between them is not so great as to defeat comprehension or to make communication and responding impossible, any more than the difference between their bodies makes you wonder whether they belong to the same species or not.

So although the sexual drive takes a different form in men from that which it takes in women, and although it differs considerably from person to person, it is safe to assume that every person who comes to The Samaritans has some sexual need. Whether this sexual need is being severely frustrated, in which case that is the problem that has brought the person, whether he admits it in the first interview or not, or whether he is doing quite nicely in this respect, thank you, never forget that any human body you meet – even if he or she does not appear very attractive erotically to yourself – is a person who has sexual needs which are not to be underestimated or considered unimportant.

If you think of sexual gratification as the need for pleasurable sensations in the body culminating in an orgasm, then you are thinking of something where frustration need not be long continued. It is only when you begin to think of the sexual needs of a human being in broader terms than the needs of the animal body that you recognise the components of the frustration which are more difficult to meet, namely the emotional components. So far as we know an animal simply wants the relief of the sexual tension which has been built up. In the case of the male animal this is by orgasm. The enjoyment of the female animal is somewhat different. When we turn to the human being there is a greater emotional need for a love relationship in both male and female than there is a physical need for an orgasm. This applies even more to the female than to the male, but it applies very much more to the male than is usually recognised, though human females need orgasm too. A large proportion of those who complain of sexual frustration and whom we are unable to help in any direct way, do nevertheless experience diminution of their sexual frustration through being befriended and thus released from their terrible obsession. What happens of course is not that their sexual difficulties or their sexual needs diminish, but that the emotional components which they were misinterpreting as physical hunger are dealt with and therefore the physical hunger is cut down to size. It may still be big and painful, but it will be less painful than when a great emotional need was being mixed up and confused with it, or interpreted as sexual frustration in the narrower sense. The person who was sexually frustrated in the *broader* sense (both physically and emotionally) was assuming that it was only physical.

Samaritan befriending can, to some extent, make up for this emotional lack: only to some extent because, of course, as one of my clients so pathetically put it, when Adam was lonely God didn't create for him ten friends, but one wife.

In dealing with clients with sexual frustration we have to realise that our befriending consists of two things: 1. recognising it as a very painful thing, not minimising it, not pretending that they ought not to suffer from it, and 2. dealing with the component of this frustration which we as Samaritans may deal with. We are not permitted to deal with the purely physical side of the need of the clients. So the befriending we are able to give only deals with a fraction of the need; but half a loaf or a quarter of a loaf is better than no bread, and the other components of sexual frustration are very much easier to bear and to cope with if you have friends who sympathise and who do give you such affection as it is right for them to give. Even if you find cases where the client becomes so fond of you and is so grateful for your friendship that he or she longs for some erotic expression of this and is disappointed because it is not possible in the Samaritan relationship to engage in this at all, nevertheless his or her disappointment that you are unable to give expression to your affection in this particular way does not, in the majority of cases, destroy the value of the friendship. The client would rather have a friend of whom he or she would like more than can be given, than not to have a friend. And to have someone who loves you and says, 'No – sorry', is a less unhappy situation than to be alone and disregarded, surrounded by jostling strangers some of whom might well say 'Yes' to this particular question but 'No' to any genuine care or long-term concern.

As far as purely physical components of sexual frustration are concerned, these can in both sexes be dealt with otherwise than in the context of a love relationship of a mutual kind, which is obviously the ideal. Of course, what most of us want is a relationship of mutual love of which sex is part of the expression. But if we are thinking of the physical component, and of those who have not chosen either to deny this appetite or to divert their energies into other channels, there is still the possibility of dealing with the purely physical side of their need by their own efforts in masturbation. In some cases they obtain gratification of their physical need with someone who does not love them – who indeed, if a prostitute, may hate and despise them, or, if a frigid wife, is simply unresponsive and not very willing. In some cases they are able to obtain the satisfaction of the physical side of their need in a context which is quite unacceptable, such as that of a married homosexual whose physical relationship with his wife does give, if he is able to have it, some relief. Similarly the case of the lesbian married to a heterosexual male. But whether they obtain relief by masturbation or by some form of sexual activity which is not really what the person wants, there is no justification for supposing that sexual frustration is predominantly of this physical kind, because nearly everybody who experiences the urgent need for orgasm is able to procure one by some means or other, even if they have not the kind of love relationship they want.

One of the things we are able to do in The Samaritans is to enable people not to think badly of themselves when they are driven to these various measures in order to release an unbearable tension, and thus allow them to be free of the obsession, allow them to get their minds on to something else. The way to do it is to be very permissive and unsurprised and to take it as a matter of course when they mention (if they mention – if you are proved worthy to have it mentioned to you) the various ways in which they make their difficult life a little less unbearable. Here Samaritan befriending comes in again. I have noticed cases where a person has come to me for sexual counselling and was not apparently being very much comforted. Considerably *helped*, unless I flatter myself, by having certain things sorted out, but not really terribly comforted by the fact that I accepted his sado-masochistic visit once in three months to a prostitute, for which he despised himself, or his 'flashing' or his pinching underwear from clothes lines, or whatever. He was not very comforted by the fact that *I* accepted this, because he said to himself, 'This man is dealing with people's sexual problems from morning to night, nothing shocks him any more', and therefore my acceptance of him did not count – though such expertise as I have did, I hope, help him. But if he is given a befriender, and can eventually bring himself to speak a little about his situation, he finds that his befriender, who is not an expert and is *not* dealing with this subject morning, noon and night, accepts it in the same casual, matter of fact, understanding way, then he is comforted.

Just as we often find that in matters of religion the testimony of a layman counts for so much more than the testimony of a parson, who may be believed to have an axe to grind, so in this matter the non-psychiatric or non-counselling person, namely the Samaritan befriender, can give much comfort. He is not shocked or horrified and just understands that people have their needs: some are lucky in being able to gratify them in a socially and religiously acceptable way and some are unlucky that they cannot. Instead of suffering from too great feelings of guilt or of anxiety, the client is able to accept himself as a person who in a difficult situation is doing the best he can, God knows. If you compare the total gratification that he has with that obtained by people no more meritorious than himself who just happen to be happily married, you can see he lives on a very thin, frugal ration, and to start begrudging him what little he does have would be un-Samaritan in the extreme. The reason why we seek to enable him so to conduct his life that he is able to form love relationships, which may or may not include some sexuality, is not because we want to get him out of his 'wicked practices' but because we know that the gratification he has found in whatever it is he has to do, is very poor compared with that which God meant him to have, and which he could have in the context of the love relationship. It is not that we, like the general public, think of the people with their various deviations, counterfeits, substitutes and whatnot as being a reprehensible lot who are having a wonderful time. We feel rather that here is an example of the terrible truth, 'To him that hath shall be given; from him that hath not shall be taken away even that which he hath'.

It seems so unfair that those who have found love should not only have the deepest need of the human being satisfied by finding love, but should also get a hundred times more out of their sex than those who have nothing but sex, either from a professional or from themselves or in some context which is not satisfying to them. When such deprived ones feel that we are not wanting to spoil what little satisfaction or relief they are able to find for themselves, but are ambitious for them to find something better if they can, then they are ready to accept our help. When clients realise that our concern is that they should live life to the full, that they should have the opportunity to gratify their sexual needs in the wider sense of their need for love, for mutual love and not a mere passing physical spasm, then they sit up and take notice.

It is not so much what we say that counts: it is our whole attitude. And if they sense that we are sorry, that we are compassionate, that we accept them, that we wish them very well, and that we want to give them what we can of our own love, then we shall really be doing a good job of Samaritan befriending in cases of sexual frustration.

Homosexual problems

W. Lawton Tonge

Homosexuality is a common phase of emotional development in early adolescence in both sexes. We are all affected by it even if it is not given physical expression. Nearly 40 per cent of the men interviewed by Kinsey in the 1940s could recall a homosexual experience. This must be affected by circumstances; it is more likely to occur in a residential school for boys or girls only, and less likely in a co-educational atmosphere. Whether the youngster has a homosexual experience or not is probably less important than his attitude to it. Adults who are in charge of him should react without anxiety, then he may mature into heterosexual relationships without difficulty. Homosexual activity at thirteen certainly doesn't imply a lifelong inversion. For some boys and girls, however, this can be a very testing experience. In spite of the reassurance of rational attitudes from the adult world, some young people can be full of guilt and depression at the thought that such impulses lie within them. Adolescence is an emotionally unstable age, and the problem of homosexuality can bring some of them to despair and thoughts of suicide. If a simple talking out of the problem does not bring relief, then expert help is needed – to deal with the depression, I should add, rather than with the homosexuality.

Only about 4 per cent of men (the figures for women are less certain) stay homosexual. The cause for this is not clearly known. Some authorities have believed the cause to be genetic, but the evidence is not satisfactory. There is certainly no evidence that these people are different from others in physical build or in hormones. Psychological factors must play a part, and most research reports describe the homosexual as typically having a poor relationship with a weak, inadequate or absent father. The mothers are often dominant. Nevertheless, not all homosexuals have this background, and many who are not homosexuals come from families which are disturbed in this way. An early initiation into homosexual behaviour cannot be blamed. One investigation reports such a seduction in both heterosexual and homosexual men.

If the causes are uncertain, treatment (for those who desire it) is not much better. Reports from psychotherapists are conflicting, but in many cases it would be unrealistic to promise a change even if psychotherapy was generally available. Behaviour therapy is still being evaluated, and one of my colleagues has been getting promising results in about a quarter of the patients whom he treated. The results are affected by the degree of inversion. Some men are more strongly homosexual than others, and treatment promises less to this group. It would appear as if 1 homosexual in 25 spontaneously becomes heterosexual.

It would seem, therefore, that the task of the counsellor is to help the homosexual to come to terms with his or her constitution.

The reasons why homosexuals seek help are important. The reform of the law regarding male homosexuals has not altered their need for help, except for the group which formerly were sent for treatment only by the Court. These are no longer seen.

In the first place there are the homosexuals who are disgusted with themselves. They regard homosexuality not as a naturally occurring condition, but as an evil or diseased thing inside themselves which they wish to get rid of. In some one receives the impression that they would be happier without any sexual feeling at all. Even if one could carry out this wish, I do not think it would help because their real disorder lies in their conflict with themselves and with their nature. Healing comes from reconciliation, not from the victory of conscience over sexuality, even if the sexuality is deviant.

Any homosexual who seeks help is liable to be in trouble with himself, and also because he lives in a society which is organised for a different pattern of sexual behaviour from his own. No homosexual, however well balanced, can fail to feel that he belongs to a persecuted minority. Advertisements are directed at men with different sexual inclinations. Even without being malicious, his married colleagues tend to exploit his single status, expecting him to be flexible when it comes to arranging holiday periods or unpopular spells of duty. 'He hasn't a family, so he won't mind' – as if he did not have a private life either. Many feel that their inversion is a secret to be jealously guarded, fearing, not without reason, that they would lose friends and respect if their condition were to be made public. The danger of being labelled as an outcast from society leads to a terrible isolation. These men need befriending, to have someone to talk to who will not reject them once the secret is confessed. This is a special problem in the North for younger homosexual men.

The greatest hazard of the homosexual, and the one that

leads to suicide, is their spiritual loneliness. It could be argued that now that the law has been reformed, that there is no reason why a homosexual should not share his life with a friend, and enjoy much of the comfort and companionship of marriage except for children. Indeed, one study of homosexual men showed that 50 per cent of them had a stable relationship (compared with 72 per cent of the heterosexuals who were married) and the rate of infidelity wasn't much higher (33 per cent and 42 per cent).

Any account of marriage which claims to have some degree of psychological sophistication has to account for conflict between the partners, not in the sense that this is an unavoidable imperfection, but as a necessary stimulus for the growth into maturity. It seems likely that this is true for all two-person relationships. We must assume that the same is true for homosexual relationships. There have been times when I have suspected that the relationship between two homosexuals contains a fiercer destructiveness than that which is found in heterosexual relationships, but I must not mislead you with what after all may be chance observations. To say that the homosexual relationship is no better than marriage is to say enough.

Consider now all the forces which prevent the break-up of a marriage, the common investment in children and home, the socio-economic dependence of the wife, the pressure of opinion. None of these apply to the homosexual couple. It would be surprising if these relationships were not in danger of flying apart, and many homosexuals live in dread of losing the person they love. What are they to do if one of them is offered an attractive post in another part of the country? This is a hard enough problem for a marriage. The homosexual couple rarely achieve an emotional security comparable to that provided by marriage.

Not every homosexual achieves a stable relationship. A proportion (no one knows how many) rely entirely on promiscuous contacts, and this would seem to apply especially to the homosexuals who have failed to come to terms with their condition. No existence is more lonely than that of these men. They live alone in a flat, and all their spare time is spent in searching for a contact. When they find someone the relationship lasts only for days or weeks; often it is for that night only. Searching for love they find only sex, and the risk of prosecution for importuning in public. As they grow older they fear (with some reason) that they will find it harder to secure new partners. Most homosexuals seem to prefer younger men, who are symbols of the idealised masculinity which is slipping from their grasp. They know in their hearts that their quest will end in failure. They retire to their rooms and turn to the anaesthesia of alcohol or suicide.

Although many homosexuals make a contented and useful adjustment to society, the gloomy picture which I have painted is no exaggeration for some. They are men very much at risk in our society, and in need of help and befriending.

Marital problems

The focus of my view of marriage is on *communication*. In a healthy marriage there is a constant, bubbling exchange of words, ideas, feelings. Sometimes this is expressed in conversation, sometimes in shared activities either of work or recreation, sometimes in gifts or services, the unasked-for courtesies which people who are in love do for each other, sometimes it is in rows and often in love making. All these things, and others, are happening constantly. The channels of communication are never empty. Even in sleep they lie touching each other.

In this process all that is good and all that is bad is brought up for the partner's inspection and acceptance. This includes weakness and inadequacy, impatience and irritability, selfishness and laziness. There must be one person in one's life with whom one can be unreasonable and petty. Always to be reasonable and mature is to pretend, and pretence is a poison to a genuine relationship. Naturally this does not take place without some friction and hurt, but my point is that these are not imperfections of an otherwise ideal marriage, but part of the necessary toil in a workshop. If there are none of these signs, then one may suspect that whatever is going on, a marriage is not being forged.

How then should one define pathology in marriage? In my view this consists of blocked or distorted communications. Silence, or the chatter which conceals silence; rows in which the real protests are concealed and not brought forth; lack of agreement in common matters such as money or the discipline of children; lack of satisfaction in the sexual relationship.

At this point I should make it clear that even the physical sexual problems of marriage are best understood in terms of a disturbed emotional relationship between the couple. I must admit that there are individuals who are in difficulties with their bodies, and this gives rise to sexual problems. There are young women, for example, whose marriages are not consummated, and who behave as if their bodies lacked genital organs. Yet these difficulties are overcome with a little help if there is a normal emotional relationship between the couple. Where such difficulties persist and lead to despair, one may rightly suspect that the sexual inhibitions are being made use of to express emotional difficulties. One woman for example, after her husband had failed to penetrate, thought to herself with glee, 'I've kept him off again'. These are more than sexual difficulties; they are an expression of an enduring if unconscious hostility towards the partner. It is the hate inside the woman which makes intercourse painful, not a disorder of her anatomy.

The same applies to men. Impotence and premature ejaculation may amount to a failure to give, a failure in loving, in more than one sense of that phrase. The barriers may be anger, guilt, a fear of hurting or sometimes quite simply a demonstration of the truth (which the individual does not dare acknowledge openly) that there is no love.

W. LAWTON TONGE

Alcoholism and the layman

Norman Ingram-Smith

The alcoholic is a person who comes under some form of *compulsion* in his drinking. There are five different kinds of alcoholic. Of these, I will discuss three, one at either end of the scale and one in the middle. The man in the street imagines an alcoholic to be an elderly man with three or four days' growth of beard and a long overcoat. He may have a bottle of surgical spirit or V.P. wine in his pocket. This ancient man of the bomb-site is indeed an alcoholic, but he is probably other things as well. He is likely to be a psychopath; he may be in a psychotic condition most of the time and it is very unlikely that the multiplicity of things that are wrong with him can be corrected in the remaining portion of his life. I would not say that he is beyond help, but he is probably a crude spirit drinker, which demands highly specialised assistance.

At the other end of the scale is the more common type of alcoholic – the businessman. There are numerous businessmen who are alcoholics; they are very rarely drunk, but they are also very rarely sober. They are in a kind of 'topped-up' state. You would not know that they were alcoholic unless alcohol was withdrawn from them altogether. If the businessman has a car accident and is taken to hospital, he may be found to be in a great state of discomfort, his hands may be shaking badly. This is nothing to do with the accident but is a manifestation of withdrawal symptoms. Such people have reached the stage where they require a regular ingestion of alcohol to be able to survive.

Between these two extremes is the bout drinker. He is difficult to deal with because he does not always manifest the known symptoms. Bout drinkers may not drink at all between bouts, they may not like alcohol, and they may normally drink very little. For several months they may drink nothing, and then will suddenly take alcohol with the most disastrous effects. They may recover consciousness at the end of a bout in a police cell, charged with theft, without any recollection of how it had happened. It is difficult to cope with the bout drinker, because it is extremely hard for him to realise that he is an alcoholic.

We must make alcoholics realise that it is better to be an alcoholic than it is to be a drunk. If I get drunk and beat someone up the fact remains that I could have stopped before I got to that pitch. It is a question of morals: it was my own choice. If I were an alcoholic, a harmless pint of beer would activate the illness. After the first drink there would be very few moral considerations left, my ability to choose would have gone.

Alcoholics are usually immature people, and show a lot of the characteristics of people who have sexual illnesses of one kind or another. The process through which they have to go, the curative process, is largely one of maturing. You have to help them to mature. When an alcoholic is not drinking he is packed with guilt because he knows that he has done things when drunk which he would not have done when sober. Connected with guilt is remorse, when a person looks back and says that if he had not been drinking, he might have been this, that or the other. Suspicion is another problem. For the alcoholic, there are usually only three things other people are interested in: his money, his body or his alcohol. He is thus suspicious of your friendship, and it is most important when dealing with an alcoholic that you give some explanation for your friendship.

People drink today because they are over-stimulated: the ordinary kind of stimuli of life are no longer sufficient. We are an alcoholic community, and certain unfortunate people carry our symptoms. It is commonly said that there are about 300,000 to 500,000 alcoholics in this country, but it is more likely there are 700,000 to 1,000,000, largely because the women are hidden. I believe there are more alcoholic women than men, although it is said that the men/women ratio of alcoholics is 3:1.

What can we, as lay folk, do about this problem? We can persuade alcoholics to have treatment. This is most important. It is no good telling an alcoholic he can be cured: he can't; but he can get better. He can learn to live his life without taking alcohol at all. He cannot play about with social drinking.

How do you recognise an alcoholic? You can ask him a few dates. If questioned about the date of his divorce he will be uncertain of the exact year or month, but will remember clearly the circumstances in which he first tasted alcohol, the date and the hour. His first drink was significant, but his divorce and his wedding meant nothing.

Very often the rigid abstainer is a person who is a born alcoholic and totally abstains because of this. He doesn't realise this of course, and thus the first drink is very significant.

Those are two ways in which you can spot an alcoholic. The National Council on Alcoholism can supply a list of similar questions, such as: does he need a drink in the morning after a night of drinking? Does he get the shakes? Does he ever take alcohol instead of eating a meal?

The community's ignorance accounts for a lot of alcoholism, and accounts for people not seeking treatment at an early stage. Alcoholism is not just super-drunkenness. Some alcoholics are rarely, if ever, drunk. An alcoholic damages himself, his social life, and his commercial life by taking alcohol when he doesn't want to, knowing that the damage is done through alcohol.

This is a distinct disease. An alcoholic, when he drinks, undergoes a change of personality. He does things which he would not dream of doing, on principle and by habit, when sober. Interestingly, the personality change seems always to be for the worse, never for the better.

The community must know that this is a disease which requires treatment. It is much better to be an alcoholic than an old drunk, as you can do something about it.

There should be no separate code for the alcoholic man and the alcoholic woman. If a man keeps an alcoholic wife at home everybody thinks he is noble, but if a woman keeps a drunken husband at home everybody thinks she is foolish. The man is very often turned out of the home and he may go for treatment, but the woman is more often protected, and therefore kept away from treatment. Consequently, when she is driven to have some form of treatment she has deteriorated so badly that she is almost beyond help. A woman suffers more, physically, under alcohol than does a man, but no one openly admits that women have drinking problems.

Alcoholics must be encouraged to go for treatment. If

you are an employer do not sack people because they are alcoholics who are now dried out. An alcoholic I knew went for an interview with a very big engineering company. He had all the qualifications and the right experience, but the interview wasn't going too well. The interviewer, who was a director of the firm, was sure he had met the man somewhere before. They went out to lunch together, and came back to finalise the interview. My friend was doubtful about getting the job and decided he might as well tell the interviewer the truth. It turned out that the interviewer had been leaving the alcoholic unit, treated, as my friend was just arriving, roaring drunk.

Social effects of alcoholism

In the family setting, alcoholism produces a markedly disruptive effect. The alcoholic becomes progressively isolated from his, or her, family: the family make considerable efforts to keep the alcoholic inside the family circle: ultimately, the process breaks down and the alcoholic is left outside the family circle, which re-forms without him.

The family feel considerable guilt about the process and feel that if they had only done this, that, or the other thing that the process of separation would never have happened. In fact it is neither the patient's fault, nor the family's fault: it is what happens in this condition unless the patient adapts to stop drinking alcohol. Since only a certain percentage of alcoholic patients do succeed in stopping drinking, the need for social work with the family in this situation is evident.

Having dealt with four or five years of increasing inefficiency in which she has taken over an increasing load of responsibilities in the family, the wife is faced after a relatively short period of recovery by a husband who is looking to resume his place in the house. If the patient recovers, the wife needs help in adjusting to the new circumstance: this period of adjustment may well take a year. If he does not improve and if drinking continues, she needs help in increasing her independence.

This is a wide field for the Samaritans who may be involved with the patient or family at different stages of the illness.

In social life, the alcoholic becomes isolated. The happy man with the pint pot surrounded by admiring friends in the advertisement may be the lot of the social drinker: the alcoholic becomes progressively isolated and in doing so takes more drink in order to feel less isolated, which in turn makes his condition worse. Whatever one can say of the personality of the alcoholic before he or she is addicted, part of the response to the addictive process is for the patient to become more dependent and passive, allowing others to do things for him.

PATRICK MULLIN

Treatment of the alcoholic

After the initial withdrawal phase the alcoholic patient is helped to adapt to an alcohol-free life, which will not be a problem-free life. The diganosis is discussed with him, and its implications. The management of drinking situations which he will face, the management of his often very disrupted family situation, are discussed with him. He is told about the management of a relapse if it should occur and about the use of the follow-up service and the use of voluntary bodies such as Alcoholics Anonymous, the Council on Alcoholism and The Samaritans' service. His resources are mobilised and he is got to work in dealing with his alcoholism. In the follow-up direction and support are needed. The slow recovery of the narcotic addicts that are now seen has given some insight into the recovery of the alcoholic. I used to think the alcoholic fortunate in that he could look forward to definite improvement in his work and family situation in as little a time as a month 'dry' and out of hospital. In fact it takes a much longer period than this to restore damaged self-confidence.

One particular person to look out for is the alcoholic who has taken an excessive amount of alcohol over many years – say, 30 or 40 years of taking a bottle of whisky a day or more. Symptoms of alcoholism may develop, or some other circumstance happen, and the patient stops drinking. His recovery period is, I think, much more arduous than in the average alcoholic and his self-knowledge at the beginning of the period of recovery may be very slight indeed. These patients tend to become depressed and need more support than the others.

The results of treatment of alcoholism tend to show that about 50 per cent of patients improve: either entirely off alcohol, or going through crisis periods, perhaps relapsing, and then remaining off alcohol again. I think that male industrial workers tend to have particularly poor results and that it is worth concentrating on this group and improving their result.

PATRICK MULLIN

Drug dependence

I am against the legalisation of pot for two reasons. Firstly I am convinced from talking to students that it takes away some of the resolve to study: their examination results tend to decline. Secondly the more I talk to these people, the more

I am impressed by the fact that their smoking is an attempt to escape from reality. They indulge in this drug as they and others do in alcohol, especially when under stress.

In some way anti-depressant drugs enable people to cope with the difficulties of life without the need to fly to the more escapist drugs. But are we to contemplate a future society in which an appreciable proportion of people can only carry on if they are continuously on drugs? Is it not more reasonable to ask ourselves whether the structure of society should remain in such a state that it generates more and more disturbed people?

IVOR MILLS

Helping the addict

To be dependent on something socially disapproved, injurious to health, and difficult to obtain, is an unenviable situation. Since the continuance of the use of it satisfies, temporarily, an urgent need, it is often more intolerable to parents, partners, friends or Samaritans, than to the one who is being harmed or committing slow suicide. The temptation to try to impose a decision to 'kick it' must be resisted, as this will be frustrating and unrewarding on both sides and probably force the addict to lie about drug abuse and eventually be caught out and scolded or rejected.

The addict, unless markedly psychopathic (as many are), needs a friend who accepts him or her *with* the addiction, who is willing to give moral support to any efforts the sufferer may freely choose to make, and to whom failure may be as readily confided as success. When the addict decides to seek a cure, only a Drug Addiction Clinic will do.

CHAD VARAH

Loneliness

W. Lawton Tonge

However we may wish to define mental health, there is one fact which cannot be denied about healthy people: they are continuously supported in a network of personal relationships. Conversely, the lives of suicides and would-be suicides show to a greater or lesser degree an interruption or disturbance of their relationships. These relationships can of course be broken in many ways and for many reasons.

Loneliness is one facet of this problem. It implies some degree of interpersonal failure. Usually, when speaking of loneliness, most people are thinking of social, that is physical, isolation. 'I have no one to talk to . . .' the clients complain. This is a very real problem, especially for the old and for strangers. If one has survived the death of friends and family, there may be literally no one left with whom there are any bonds of friendship. Equally distressing is the plight of younger people who have immigrated to a city and spend long hours in the bed-sitter. It is well known that such situations predispose to suicide. Sainsbury, for example, found that suicide was much more common amongst the unemployed, lodging-house keepers and domestic servants.

This is not just a question of social class: according to the Registrar-General, miners share the lowest suicide rate, together with clergymen.

Sainsbury then studied the way of life, and found that nearly a third of his suicides were living alone, and over a fifth lived in boarding houses: and these are much higher proportions than in the general population of London. This suggested that isolation, loneliness and not-belonging were perhaps important motives for suicide. This would explain why lonely occupations, such as domestic service and lodging-house keeping, have high suicide rates, while occupations which bring men into close contact with each other, such as miners and the clergy, have low suicide rates.

In order to check this hypothesis, Sainsbury examined those London boroughs which had high suicide rates, and compared them with boroughs with low suicide rates. As one might expect, he found that in boroughs with a high suicide rate there was a much increased proportion of persons living alone, especially living in one room and in hotels and lodgings. They also had a greater number of immigrants, and a greater number of people born outside London. The rates for divorce and illegitimacy were also higher where suicide was prevalent. The facts are no longer in dispute: to be exposed to the stress of isolation and loneliness increases the risk of suicide.

Faced with this situation, it is obvious that our response must be to meet this need, in so far as we are able. In our own clinic we became disturbed by this plight of older women living on their own, and we started a social club for them. Although it was only possible for the club to meet once a week, the response on the part of our patients was most gratifying: their need to attend hospital or have treatment as in-patients fell off markedly. Depression was the most common and severe symptom, but our simple institution, undemanding in time and money for its organisers, now makes some contribution to the prophylaxis of suicide for this socially underprivileged population.

For the same reason, it is no coincidence that the volunteers in The Samaritans are called 'befrienders'. Human beings need the support of friendly relationships as surely as they need food and water, and deprivation in this respect can lead equally to a fatal result. There are few of us who, at some time or other in our life, are not tempted to despair and suicide, and the knowledge that there is someone who cares for us is a strong barrier to the impulses of self-destruction. The provision of this friendly support must therefore be one of the major concerns of any organisation which is engaged in the prevention of suicide.

But I am convinced that neither a supply of befrienders, however generous, nor the provision of social clubs, is an adequate answer to the problem of human loneliness. Loneliness not as a social fact but as an inner experience is a word with more than one meaning.

The experience of loneliness is probably inseparable from life as we know it today. Indeed loneliness in the form of privacy is a very highly rated commodity. At least in this country we pay extra for houses which are completely detached from our neighbours', for gardens which cannot be overlooked. For many holiday-makers, the perfect beach is one which is devoid of any other people. This is one aspect of contemporary culture which is in marked contrast with earlier times. Paul Halmos, in his study of solitude and privacy, quotes Rosamund Bagne-Powell: 'We must remember that overcrowding was characteristic of the age. Well-to-do people thought little of . . . two sleeping in a bed. The pupils at expensive boarding schools were herded together under the most insanitary conditions. Servants slept in the kitchen or lay on the staircase and passages. Travellers at inns would share rooms and beds with total strangers. Privacy did not seem to be valued even by those who could insist upon it.'

There were, of course, many good practical reasons for this avoidance of solitude; by and large it was dangerous. Public security could not be taken for granted as it is today. Moreover, the whole structure of feudal society demanded that one should be placed in a certain station in life, to which one was bound with duties and privileges, and from which there was no escape. To rise in the world, as we know it, was unthinkable, and to be an independent operator was madness. As Lewis Mumford puts it: 'The unattached person during the middle ages was one either condemned to exile or doomed to death: if alive, he immediately sought to attach himself, at least to a band of robbers. To exist, one had to belong to an association: a household, a manor, a monastery, a guild: there was no security except in association, and no freedom that did not recognise the obligations of a corporate life. One lived and died in the style of one's class and corporation.' But today this solitude which we seek may also be the loneliness which we fear. It represents a need which is also a hazard characteristic of our times.

The meaning of this loneliness is most clearly marked out in the case of a young woman who consulted me in depression and despair. Her temperament was that of a lively, careless, extroverted person. Her parents were careful middle-class people who hoped above all that their daughter would hold a steady and respectable job in some sort of secretarial capacity which would be completely in conformity with the family tradition. Loyally, this girl had sought to live up to the expectations of her family, but found that she was en-circled by a sense of frustration and despair. Her friends, most of whom shared the outlook of her parents, could not fathom the cause of her unhappiness. When pressed, she admitted that it was her secret ambition to work as a recep-tionist in an hotel or club, but she felt she did not dare mention this at home because it was so contrary to her parents' ambitions for her; likewise her friends would not understand. She felt lonely, deserted and in despair, and yet I would not hesitate to diagnose this as a neurotic problem.

I have dwelt at some length on this somewhat everyday example because I think it illustrates clearly a characteristic-ally contemporary dilemma. The need for self-determina-tion, the right to control one's own affairs, is highly valued in our culture, whether for individuals or for nations. Yet this decision demands more or less a break with the past. Old ways may have to be rejected. This can lead to great feelings of loneliness, and is a sort of separation anxiety: the spiritual equivalent of the panic which small children feel when they cry out for their mother and get no reply. In much the same way the young people of our society cry out for guidance and are met by the silence of moral condemna-tion or the exhortation to work things out for themselves. I suggest therefore that the struggle for emotional maturity inevitably brings about some degree of loneliness. One has lost touch with the older generation, and one's own genera-tion has yet to find an answer. There is no one to turn to.

But there are other and more intractable forms of loneli-ness than the isolation of an individual in a crisis of self-determination. I see loneliness essentially as the consequence of a breakdown in the emotional transactions between people. The most impenetrable isolation is when the person concerned finds himself unable to enter into an emotional commitment, notwithstanding an intense desire to do so. Such people find themselves lonely although surrounded by friends and family. Perhaps married, they find themselves committed to a life of pretending to feelings which they do not experience, and, which is the more bitter, because they have to simulate feelings which they ardently wish to be real. When faced with this type of loneliness, it is tempting to ascribe it to circumstances; thus some women imagine that a lover would be more successful than their husband in breaking down their inner reserve; some unmarried men believe that their failure to marry is because they do not move in the right social circles, and so on. But in their innermost hearts they know these thoughts to be but rationalisations, and that a crystal wall, transparent and infrangible, effectively seals their hearts against those who could love them.

This is a neurotic situation which responds, if at all, to psychotherapy, and I believe it is beyond the reach of counselling or befriending. However, the act of befriending, although powerless to shatter their invisible defences against love, does something to relieve the acute sense of loneliness and frustration which these neurotics suffer. To know that someone is trying to get through induces a pathetic gratitude, although the result is known to be useless.

This is not the time or place to discuss in any depth the psychopathology of these conditions, but it must be remarked that in many of these cases, underneath a façade of friendliness and sophistication is a deep mistrust. A typical comment from one of my patients was that he had learned not to pray to God because if he made his wants known, that would make sure they would be refused. Such people are often generous as regards their belongings, and their time, provided that they are not personally involved. In their own deepest needs, they are unable to give and are therefore often frigid or impotent in their sexual relationships. Although desperately wanting the love of others, their fear of involvement closes their eyes to the opportunities for love relationships which are presented to them. They are constantly exposed to humiliations when they see others, less talented, to be more successful both in love and work.

The same difficulties and frustrations attend their treatment. Although they make conscientious patients, they never really trust the therapist, and complain that he does not offer the help to which they are entitled. They are quick to take offence and do not believe that their therapist is really concerned for them. These invisible barriers are very hard to break, and bring humiliation to the patient and frustration to the therapist.

Although the situation which I have described is fortunately rare, I believe that minor varieties of this difficulty are common enough in many who complain of loneliness. Behind the rationalisation of lack of social contact and bad luck, one can dimly perceive the scared and humiliated ego which draws back at every attempt on the part of others for a closer relationship. In their hearts these people live in a barren, deserted and hostile world.

Bereavement

C. Murray Parkes

The effects of bereavement

In considering the effects of a bereavement, I think there are four main areas that we have to consider. There is *grief* itself – that is to say the psychological reaction to the loss. There are the effects of *deprivation*. For instance, a woman who loses her husband not only suffers from the loss of her husband, but she also has to learn to live without him. She is, from then onwards, a person without a husband. She suffers not only loss but psychological starvation. Then there is the *role change* that accompanies most losses – the fact that being a married woman, for instance, is not the same thing at all as being a widow. A person in one situation in life has to learn a new set of roles. Attached to this is the way in which this change in role is perceived by society, particularly in the case of many losses the *stigma* which is associated with the loss. Here again, one can think in terms of loss of a person, or one can think in terms of other types of loss. For instance, an amputee – someone who loses a limb – is undoubtedly stigmatised – he becomes the recipient of sympathy. Sympathy is a very belittling thing. It is very damaging to self-respect. It's a stigma. When I say stigma I don't just mean the negative hostile element which undoubtedly does creep in, but also the way in which people are frightened and embarrassed by those who are closely associated with loss, particularly where a death is involved. Every widow discovers that there are certain people who find it very difficult to talk to her, who feel somehow threatened by her, and they react in an embarrassed way. This implies that there is a form of stigma. It's less obvious in our society than in many others where the widow may come under quite severe taboos for a period after her bereavement. In one island in the Philippines the widow is not allowed to see or speak to anybody. She walks through the forest with a stick which she taps on trees to warn people that she is coming, and it is believed that even the trees she touches will die, so closely is the widow associated with the death of the person whom she survives. The same fears exist in our civilisation and I think they account for some of the tendency to ignore, avoid and blind ourselves to the needs of bereaved people.

The process of grieving

There are several factors which determine whether a person goes through the process of grieving in a healthy manner or develops one of these abnormal reactions. I think there are three main things to be considered: there is the nature of *the relationship with the dead person* and other factors influencing the magnitude of the grief itself. Here I put two things first, dependence and ambivalence. Where the relationship has been a very dependent one where the widow or widower has been highly involved to the point that her whole life centred on the other person – she is particularly liable to develop a severe reaction after the loss. There is also the opposite type of relationship. The husband and wife have quarrelled a great deal and perhaps there have been times when one has actually wished the other one dead. When death wishes are gratified the survivor has a tremendous load of guilt to make up. One of the things that sometimes happens is that the survivor will do a complete about-turn and say 'I was always quarrelling with my husband, but now I realise he was right'. In order to try to put this right she will spend the rest of her life in mourning for him. There are, of course, other forms which this ambivalent attitude can take.

The second main determinant is the effect of *defence* – the defences of the bereaved person against pain and distress. Now, we all know people who are very good at defending – very good at not facing up to unpleasant fact. We know families, too, where a 'stiff upper lip' is something which is a pride. 'People don't cry in our family.' So this isn't only a personal thing, it's a cultural factor. In fact there are many cultures which place very high value on the ability to control emotions and not to break down or to cry in situations which one would expect would give rise to this. Among the widows whom I was talking about earlier, those who showed the least emotion during the first fortnight of bereavement were uniformly more disturbed three months later than the rest. It appears that one can postpone grief, but one can't deny the need to grieve. Sooner or later it will break through, and that's why defending oneself in this way doesn't seem to be a satisfactory answer to the problem of grief.

Finally, I would like to mention the effects on the rehabilitation of the widow of *the environment* in which she finds herself, and here I would put social isolation as the commonest cause of trouble. If a person has a close warm family who stand by her at the time of bereavement, then she will find during the course of the next few years that there is something left in life, that there are people who can share her grief, and people who can bring her out of it. Socially isolated people tend to get 'stuck' with the chronic type of grief. Rather less common, but also a problem that can arise, is the bereaved person who is over-protected. The tendency for the family to take over is perhaps not a bad thing at first, but in time can tend to be unhealthy, if it goes on after the period when the widow would normally have found herself a job, gone out, and so on. This is particularly the case where there are young unmarried daughters at home who are willing to take over a large part of the role of the widow. We all know the situation that can arise here.

*   *   *

Grief work

The most important thing Samaritans can do to help someone who has suffered a severe bereavement is to encourage them to do what has come to be called 'grief work'. This involves taking out and looking at the memories of the one who has died, whether these were good or bad, and 'working' through them a sufficient number of times for them to be accepted, assimilated, and gently put away. Nothing prevents a bereaved person from readjusting to life more than the selfish habit of most of their relatives and friends of frustrating this need by changing the subject. They pretend this is for the mourner's good, but it is to protect themselves from embarrassment or boredom. We Samaritans are willing to assist patiently with 'grief work'.

CHAD VARAH

How ageing will affect you and me

W. B. Wright

I believe the key to success in coping with old people is to try to understand them for the human beings they are, and thoroughly appreciate their needs as such. You must not treat them as if they were some other kind of human being, but put yourself in their place, assuming that they feel essentially the same as you do, that they behave as anyone else would in their circumstances and that their needs are just the same as your needs. A day will come when you will look in the mirror and see an ancient, lined face looking back at you. On that day I believe you will feel the same within yourself, as you do now and always have done.

But think about the elderly people you have had dealings with; how out of sympathy they are with the younger generation, how narrow and conservative is their point of view on life, how bad tempered and difficult and spoilt they can be – like children, in fact. You know that the mental hospitals are more than half full of elderly people.

What is going to happen to us then, as we grow older, which is going to make us behave the way some elderly people do? First, our *thinking efficiency* will diminish. The most important component of this is memory. Memory is the ability to grasp and retain recent and remote events in the mind so that they can be recalled at will. There are two types of memory – the short-term grasp of ideas and the long-term recollection. They are quite different. If you were given a multi-digit number and asked to repeat it, you would be using your short-term memory. If you were asked to recite the seven times table, it would be your long-term memory that was being brought into play.

People vary considerably in their ability to use their recent and remote memory, but it is our grasp of new ideas which keeps us in touch with the world around us, and whereas our remote memory will remain intact, we are already losing our recent memory and grasp of ideas.

We could not now return to school and learn, afresh, the wide variety of subjects that we absorbed so easily in our early teens. We are all conscious of the lessening impact that new concepts make on us as we grow older.

This loss does not worry us as we go through life, because the more we go into our career, the more we form routines which make for smooth-running efficiency, and which incidentally spare us original thought. With ripening experience we make fewer and fewer new decisions. When confronted with a new problem we ask ourselves, 'Now, what did I do when I was last faced with a situation like this?' and everything settles itself easily. Indeed, it is this facility for which we are increasingly respected.

When a person is too old to go on with his life's work, this is not the moment to try to learn a new trade. A man may turn to the garden, but if he has never taken the trouble to take an interest in horticulture before, he may at 65 find gardening nothing but a meaningless chore. When he turns to his new book on gardening he may well find that he cannot somehow get 'into' it, and that he nods off to sleep each time he tries.

Secondly, there is *emotional balance*. As you know, our emotional balance governs to a considerable extent our enjoyment of life. Every one of us has, standing on each side of us, a caricature of ourselves. The one is full of drive, optimism and vigour – making plans for tomorrow, buckling down to the job, always ready for a party. The other is dull, pessimistic and sluggish – dreading the future, regretting the past, unable to meet the demands of the present. These are our manic and depressive sides and we stand in the middle between them, sometimes veering a little to one side or the other.

When any human being is subjected to a battery of adverse circumstances, kept up long enough and intensively enough, then his meridian can be pushed into the depressive field where it may remain even if the onslaught is withdrawn. This is what is called 'reactive depression'.

Now consider the active, industrious businessman who has devoted all his interest to his work throughout his career, and at 65 sails happily into retirement without having made any preparation for it. After what one might call the 'honeymoon period' of lying late in the mornings and taking little holiday trips, he begins to find time dragging some-what. He pays a visit to his work and meets all his old friends again, but they are all busy dealing with things that he knows nothing about, and are no longer his concern. He has no-thing to talk about except the past, and the more he tries to interest people, the more he seems to bore them. Finally he is left watching the dying embers of the fire, and his meridian moves into the depressive field. He has another 20 years of this in front of him. Furthermore, no one cares any more what he thinks or does. Suddenly the 'prop' of public expectation has been withdrawn. You have only to walk into some people's homes on a Sunday, unexpectedly, to see the degenerating effect of one day out of the public eye. Consider then what the effect of 20 years 'on the shelf' could be.

If you take the whole background into account the next time you have to deal with an elderly person, then you may find that their behaviour is just what your own behaviour would be if you were in the same circumstances.

There are two things that are as vital as material security, without which we will deteriorate. One is human contact; this is, love, friendship, companionship, to be 'in the swim', to be one of a team. The other is preoccupation; this is, adventure, a job, to be doing something absorbing, and of value. We cannot live happily or sanely for long without having these two needs satisfied.

Ageing and mental illness

The decline with ageing

In some countries, such as China and the tribal societies of Africa, the elderly are venerated as especially wise; they hold a respected place in their society. But in the West old people have long been discredited. In Biblical times age was reverenced, but the Greeks despised the physical decrepitude of the elderly, and in ancient Rome the diseases accompanying old age were emphasised.

Present medical knowledge recognises that impairment of our various physical functions starts at differing life periods. Intelligence reaches its maximum in the early twenties (although emotional maturity is attained later). The deterioration of the body begins later, causing severe wounds to the self-esteem of every person as he perceives that he has started to age. Failing of vision begins in the 40s, and some falling off in the sharpness of hearing soon after. Slowing of the thought processes is already present in middle age and can be demonstrated plainly by psychological tests. From a social point of view, old age is considered to begin at 65 for men and 60 years for women, when retirement pensions are provided.

People are often not prepared for retirement, and find themselves profoundly unprepared for their loss of employment. The mental disturbance that occurs in many people on retirement is a matter for grave concern.

Mental illness

An old person can become mentally ill in one of two ways:

1. He may have a *functional psychiatric illness*, which is the same as the emotional illnesses occurring at other ages: e.g. a depression, an anxiety neurosis or alcoholism. A serious error the doctor may make is to mis-diagnose the abnormal behaviour as due to senility; in that way emotional disorder can be overlooked which, with proper treatment, can respond well to skilled care. It is by no means uncommon to find old people in institutions with potentially recoverable conditions which unfortunately have not been diagnosed correctly and are left untreated. The need for proper medical and psychiatric services in all geriatric hospitals and homes cannot be over-emphasised. Any complaining, cantankerous old person should be investigated by a psychiatrist, who may find that the dissatisfaction with the environment is an accompaniment of a depression that can respond to appropriate treatment.

2. The second form of mental illness in the elderly is *dementia*, a loss of intellectual powers due to shrinkage of the brain with ageing. When memory impairment is so gross as to incapacitate the old person, he tends to remember events in the distant past while seriously handicapped by his failure to recall his recent experiences.

Relatives who are troubled at having to admit an aged parent to an institution can be relieved by the knowledge that with brain impairment comes a relative satisfaction with whatever environment is provided, if only it offers secure protection and responsible care. My research colleagues have found that dementing old people, as their mental powers failed, were very often perfectly contented with their circumstances, in marked contrast to old people who had the first type of psychiatric disturbance I mentioned, which is not due to brain deterioration.

H. J. WALTON

Youth and age

Erik Erikson emphasises that there may be connections between the low status of old persons in contemporary Western culture, and the lack of direction or sense of meaning that afflicts our adolescents. Erikson puts forward a concept that the generations are profoundly dependent on one another; unless the young have before them a personification of fulfilment in old age – actual evidence of respected and self-respecting old people – the young members of the community cannot develop a sense of purposeful sequence in the different phases during a lifetime. Lacking this, their own development as individuals can fail to take form and direction. The young person seeks an identity for himself, which he can be helped to find if in his society the aged have a defined place and a valued role. There is now a visible representation of each stage of life including the last. If in this sequence the elderly are overlooked or indeed actively disregarded, their neglect endangers 'the sense of life and the meaning of death' necessary for the society as a whole.

H. J. WALTON

Problems of middle-age

We, as a society, are committed to change because successful industry is committed to change. By the same token an industry not so committed is not successful and is quite likely to fail.

Youth can adapt to changes with relative ease, old age is tolerated in an increasingly kindly if formal way, but middle-age bears the brunt of enforced adaptation – at a time when many may feel tradition allows that they should begin to 'sit back'. Peter Drucker says that management must aim at challenging all to growth and self-development and that while the first demand which an enterprise makes of the worker is that he willingly directs his efforts toward the goals of that enterprise, the other great demand is that he be willing to accept change – change of his work, change of his habits, change of group relations. Rosemary Stewart describes the good manager as perceptive and flexible and suggests that therefore his experience and formal education should be planned to try to develop these qualities. Significantly, I think, she does not enlarge on how this experience and education should be planned. As Marshall McLuhan might say, the central message seems to be change – total change. The timeless experiences of life, of loving, of loss whether by disease or death, are as surely with us today as 1,000 years ago, but man has contrived changes which alter the environment in which these changes occur and I suggest that industry, while satisfying our material needs, has jeopardised the quality of emotional life which heretofore somehow cushioned these impacts. It has done this innocently but it has done it.

Business life today bristles with uncertainty and change. The sociologist Denis Pym has stated that the sort of personality nowadays required by industry is the risk-taker. Many might criticise this as too general, but it does seem that one of the requirements for adapting to industrial executive life, or professional life, is the ability to tolerate a pretty high level of uncertainty. Above all else it must be clear that industry requires very flexible people, able to adapt to new situations, new techniques, new faces, new risks. These are qualities that are more characteristic of youth, diminish in middle-age, and decline fairly sharply in old age – except in occasional individuals. Youth can take it, middle-age has to take it, old age is often exonerated. Yet middle-age is frequently the era when situations of high responsibility are demanding maximum flexibility. It should come as no surprise to us to learn that the suicide rate has in the last few decades been highest in people engaged in professional and managerial occupations, that is Class I of the Registrar-General's classification of social class. This is followed as a rule by that of businessmen and executives. Perhaps the insinuation of a Samaritan spirit into the personnel departments of organisations might introduce some modern meaning into these departments – departments for which even Peter Drucker is unable to suggest a significant role at present.

DERMOT J. WARD

The problem of the psychopath*

Richard Fox

The psychopath, as we think of him nowadays, seems to have been first recognised in 1835 as a person with a special kind of disorder who was 'incapable, not of talking, or reasoning upon any subject proposed to him, but of conducting himself with decency and propriety in the business of life'.

After much dispute the concept was enshrined in the Mental Health Act (1959) although the Scots would not have it in their equivalent Act, leaving the condition firmly within the criminal law and without a medical connotation. Our Mental Health Act defines psychopathy as a persistent disorder in a person who is *not* mentally ill, though he may be subnormal, the condition being characterised by abnormally aggressive and/or seriously irresponsible conduct. It alleges optimistically that it is susceptible to medical treatment, without rashly saying what treatment.

In women it is more likely to take the form of general (including sexual) irresponsibility than the violence shown so often by the male. The clinical features found in varying

* From a talk given at The Samaritans' National Conference, 1969.

Every kind of antisocial conduct may be shown, organised gangsterism to the petty pilferer who seems to caught every time. Irresponsible production of, and negle of, children, undertaking responsibilities and failing to see them through, malingering, intriguing, cruelty to animals – any activity repugnant to most is to be found amongst psychopaths.

Asocial

The 'loner', who never fits into the group, and is afraid of relationships.

Affectionless

Difficulty in getting emotionally close to people, of feeling any kind of genuine warmth towards others, even members of their family.

Pathological lying and plausibility

Even learned and suspicious specialists may be deceived, but people experienced in the handling of psychopaths develop a 'sixth sense' that usually helps them to spot them quickly. The lying frequently starts as a kind of fantasy over-compensation for deep-seated feelings of inferiority. A skilled psychopath may deceive his family and friends over many years, work his way into positions of responsibility, and

voc before his personality disorde
ive' aspects may be seen – perhaps as ʌ
ʌ. Lawrence. The definitive work on Hitler
Professor Mayer-Gross described him as a
psychopath.

ʒression

Aggression is common, varying from the constant bitter nastiness of, say, an unpleasant NCO to the impulsive murderer. With the impulsiveness is an inability to plan for the future: like the child who wants a bar of chocolate, he must have his wants satisfied immediately for tomorrow does not exist. Instead of dating someone for the weekend he may have to go out now, and commit rape. The pleasure-orientated nature of much of his conduct follows from this, also the selfishness.

Guiltlessness

This is especially characteristic and though deep remorse may be expressed: 'I'll never ever do it again, you have my word on that'; this is shallow, lacks sincerity, and should not convince you.

Failure to learn from experience

This leads to repetition of antisocial behaviour, with failure to respond to any kind of treatment or punishment. With the repetitiveness one finds a magical belief that they will get away with it next time, even against a long background of total ineptitude. Total lack of insight is a marked feature.

Sexual disorders

Sexual deviation, as a manifestation of personality immaturity in its own right, is very much to be expected in this particular group of people, from promiscuity and prostitution to the rare rape murderer.

Abuse of alcohol or drugs

This occurs to excess, the outlook with treatment depending on how far the subject is a true addict and how far he is psychopathic. All too often the drinking occurs as part of the general lack of emotional control and, by eroding what little inhibition the subject already has, leads to episodes of antisocial conduct that may then be wrongly blamed entirely on the alcohol.

Work instability

This is one of the commonest features. Jobs are lost through aggression, the inability to see things through, getting 'fed up', bad time-keeping, laziness, pilfering, shoddy work and so forth.

Suicidal features

Psychopaths attack the Samaritans at their weakest point, i.e. by making suicidal threats (actual suicide is uncommon and usually accidental, though as a group they *do* have an above average rate). On scrutiny these threats are seen as *manipulations* to gain some obvious end as, e.g., having debts paid off, avoiding police proceedings, trying to secure the return of a despairing spouse. Experience, again, tells one that the threat lacks sincerity but there comes a time when the personality seems to have matured to the point where violence is directed inwards instead of outwards. This can be an encouraging sign and some psychoanalysts say that you have to turn a psychopath into a neurotic before you can start to treat him!

The trouble with psychopathy as a diagnosis – unlike the psychoses discussed earlier – is that it shades off at all points into the 'normal'. While there is no agreement about the psychopath in pure culture, as it were, showing all the above features, we are most of us a *little* bit psychopathic, enough anyway to let us enjoy life. Where to draw lines between the normal and psychopathic, the helpable and unhelpable, is very difficult.

Causes of psychopathy

What makes people the way they are? Knowledge here is very incomplete. It was a big breakthrough in the 1950s when it was realised that a rare form of epilepsy arising from damage in the temporal lobes of the brain was frequently associated with aggressive personality disorder often indistinguishable from aggressive psychopathy. The EEG (brain waves) of psychopaths tend to show (though not invariably) the immature patterns of the maturing teenager which correlates nicely with the immature features of personality – selfishness, impulsiveness and so on. The role of other sorts of head injury has been much argued about, and minor forms of brain damage at, during or shortly after birth, or even during pregnancy, do sometimes seem to play some part in later behaviour disturbances. It is a feasible hypothesis that a child is thus rendered more 'vulnerable' and liable to go off the rails if things in his life do not go quite right. Psychopathic developments certainly can follow head injury in later life, but close scrutiny usually shows that the injury has but served to bring up in caricature disorders that were present before. Finally, as to physical causes, there is a rare chromosomal abnormality, the 'XYY syndrome' in which the extra male chromosome renders some subjects tall, aggressively criminal from an early age and low in intelligence.

The psychological causes, which are probably more important, are equally obscure. Family disruption with parental loss certainly plays a large part such that a child has no chance to 'learn' how to love, through being loved itself. The mother, or mother-substitute, protects the child, satisfies its needs for warmth, nourishment, relief of anxiety and so on, and if she is removed the child goes through a period of grieving. If another 'mother' appears, the child will gradually overcome this grief (expressed by infants as withdrawal, relapse into incontinence, tantrums, etc.) and come to rely in every way on this person as it did on the first. If this person is again removed – and unwanted children may experience this many times through a succession of parents, foster parents, and children's homes – the child will come to see *all* close relationships as dangerous because, inherent in them, is the threat that they will come to an end and the child will suffer grief, i.e. mental pain. He therefore 'cuts off' his emotional feelings for people. Attempts by later 'mothers' or therapists to relate to the child are met by disturbed 'testing' behaviour when the child tries to reassure itself that the 'mother' will still love it however badly it behaves, and by especial disturbance at any further threat of separation. It takes a skilled therapist to handle this kind of patient and Samaritans must beware of becoming emotionally involved with this sort of person.

Again one can see that the child who has experienced much violence in early life will give it back in adulthood in the same way that a child of loving parents is likely himself to become a secure and loving parent when his time comes. Somewhat conversely, one finds psychopaths who have apparently been indulged at every point by over-loving (often affluent) parents, who have been helped out of every scrape they have got into, and who have consequently never learned proper standards of conduct. And one finds typical cases that one just cannot account for at all.

Treatment of the psychopath

Proof of the effectiveness of medical treatment does not really exist, hence the doubts about the reference to it in the Mental Health Act definition. The old-fashioned approach was the reward/punishment system under conditions of security whereby good behaviour led to privileges and bad behaviour to loss thereof – all highly authoritarian. The technique pioneered by Maxwell Jones and practised especially at the Henderson Hospital and Grendon Prison depends upon an intensive group therapy régime, the cornerstones of which are 'peer-group judgment', i.e. it is not the authority figures (against whom the patient always rebels) but the other patients who decide what should be done. Thus selection for the Henderson Hospital is by groups of patients and punishments are decided likewise. People who are 'agin' authority respond better to the control of 'siblings' than to that of the 'parents'. Furthermore, the irresponsible are being forced into a position of responsibility. The next vital principle is that the person must be faced *at once* by the consequences of his actions – a lesson for the Samaritans here, in that they are not helping a psychopath by breaking the rules of the organisation and paying off his debts for him. Guiding him towards a rational plan for paying off his *own* debts is another matter.

Treatments by brain operation are seldom feasible. Tranquillisers can sometimes help impulsive patients over difficult phases. Impulsive aggressiveness usually seems to cease in middle age, and though a person may continue to be very abnormal and a terrible nuisance, the outlook for psychopaths does not seem to be all that different from the ordinary criminal. Some find it easier to survive within the rigid structure of institutions such as the Army or even hospital work and the espousal of a particularly rigid religious faith will sometimes help a psychopath to hold his antisocial tendencies in check. Probably the most one can offer in practice is to support the chap over crises as best one can, while he matures.

Samaritans and the psychopath

Inexperienced Samaritan branches have sometimes felt that any person who comes to them for help is deserving of all they can give, and they quote the parable of the Good Samaritan in support of this. However, what the Good Samaritan did to the man who fell among thieves was appropriate to that man's condition – he gave him treatment for his wounds and got him properly looked after until recovery. The same goes for the psychopath. What he emphatically does *not* need is Samaritan befriending plus a great deal of social help that saves him from the consequences of his own misbehaviour. This may only serve to perpetuate the pattern, and it may remove from the inadequate personality what little resources he had and make him increasingly dependent upon Samaritans, either individually or as a branch, such that his demands upon them will increase.

One branch, having failed to make a realistic assessment, spent several years trying to get a man job after job, paying off his debts, sorting out his various problems, persuading his wife to return to him (briefly) only to find at the end that their client was slightly more socially disabled than when he had first come to them. Hence the principle, always, of facing a person squarely with the consequences of his actions. A psychopath who has been allowed to develop dependency upon a branch may finally make demands which no one could meet. Samaritan branches are more vulnerable than professional workers in that anyone can wander into a branch or ring it up, and aggrieved psychopaths have been known maliciously to ring a branch every few minutes, night after night. Destructive behaviour has also occurred in branches though, happily, extremely rarely. It has even been necessary to call in the police, which Samaritans hate to have to do. For the Samaritan 'image' to become associated with that of the police or, for that matter, of the statutory mental health services, would deter many clients who could otherwise be helped.

Branches often ask what to do about the 'lame ducks'; the people who for years have found life just too difficult to cope with, the more so since they tend to bring extra burdens on themselves like unwanted children and alcoholic husbands. A limited number of such inadequate people can be given intermittent support and cups of tea up to what the Director thinks a branch's resources can tolerate, but they must not be allowed to detract from help given to the acute client. 'We're busy, come back later', said kindly, may precipitate weeping or abuse but seldom self-injury. Such people are manipulative often, but dangerous very seldom.

The problem of the psychopath

The problem, of course, is to spot early on the client for whom befriending is likely to be destructive: to the volunteer, the branch and the client himself. These decisions must be made by the leadership: the branch psychiatric consultant can be invaluable here. Early on, pending a fuller assessment, the relationship must be client–branch rather than one-to-one befriending, to protect the volunteer.

Conclusion

The problem of the psychopath is one of the most complex and intractable in the whole of psychiatry, so it is not surprising if Samaritans find this article a depressing one. It is nicer to be told when one can do good and useful work than to be made to realise that there are some for whom as yet no effective help exists. No doctor, social worker or Samaritan branch can help everybody and it is as important that we should realise our limitations as our strengths. The good that the Samaritans can do to their fellow men is immense: it has not been measured and probably never will be. So we should not allow the problem of the psychopath to discourage us.

★   ★   ★

Dangerous sentimentality

How do so many psychopaths get accepted as clients in the first place, in spite of our precautions?

They have allies within the branch. Not usually fellow-psychopaths – few of these wangle their way in, and none remains long undetected – but muddleheaded sentimentalists who can be manipulated into breaking the rules. These are as dangerous as the psychopaths, and should be eliminated promptly.   CHAD VARAH

List of Branches of The Samaritans in the United Kingdom and Eire

All the Branches offer a 24-hour-a-day service except those not in bold type. Unless otherwise stated, the Centre is *manned* 24 hours a day, so that callers can be dealt with by Samaritans who have records at hand, and more than one telephone. If calls are *transferred* for part of the 24 hours, whether to Samaritans' homes or to another Branch, the hours of manning are stated. Branches or Probationary Branches not in bold type are (at the time of writing) not giving any service for the entire 24 hours a day, but are available only at the times stated.

The number to the left of the Branch's name is its official serial number, and therefore indicates the Branch's seniority. When used on labels worn by Samaritans at inter-Branch gatherings, it should *follow* the Samaritan's own number in his or her Branch.

The initials to the right of the Branch's name, in brackets, indicate the Region to which the Branch belongs. Each full Branch elects one member to the Council of Management of The Samaritans (Inc.), and each Region elects one member to the Executive Committee of this Council.

The name in brackets after the Regional designation is that of the person responsible for the Branch at the time of going to press.

The Emergency telephone number, advertised for the use of callers seeking help, is given first, and the Office number second. The Office number will not, of course, be answered at times when the Centre is not manned, and should not be used by clients, as it may be answered by someone not a Samaritan or too busy to sound like one.

6 **Aberdeen** (Scot) (James Shearer) Aberdeen 53000 & 53990
The Samaritans, 60 Dee Street, Aberdeen AB1 2DS
Manned 09.00–07.00.

AMERSHAM – see Chilterns.

133 **Ashford** (SE) (Ivan Elgar) Ashford 24606 & 24607.
The Samaritans, 22 Beaver Road, Ashford, Kent, TN23 1RP.

70 **Ayrshire** (Scot) (David R. Bell) Kilmarnock 25353 & 24903.
Ayrshire Samaritan Service, 43 Titchfield Street, Kilmarnock, KA1 1QS.
Manned 11.00–07.00.

BANBURY – Befriending group of Oxford.

BANGOR – see North Down.

115 BARNSLEY (NE) (Douglas Drye) Barnsley 2202 & 87888.
The Samaritans, 11 Victoria Road, Barnsley, Yorks, S70 2BB.
Manned 16.00–12.00. At other times calls transferred to Sheffield.

BARNSTAPLE – see North Devon.

121 **Barrow** (NW) (Roy Punton) Barrow 25656 & 25799.
Samaritans of Furness, 138 Cavendish Street, Barrow-in-Furness, Lancs. LA14 1DJ
Manned 10.00–22.00.

87 **Basildon** (E) (Derek Butler) Basildon 22222 & 3559.
The Samaritans, 35a The Fremnells, Basildon, Essex.
Manned 11.00–23.00.

139 **Basingstoke** (S) (Ursula Barker) Basingstoke 26080 & 21039.
78 Flaxfield Road, Basingstoke, Hants.

52 **Bath** (W) (Hayes Treen) Bath 29222 & 25353.
The Samaritans, 2 New King Street, Bath, Somerset.
BA1 2BL.

37 **Bedford** (E) (Sidney Morris) Bedford 52200 & 52317.
The Samaritans, 69 Gwyn Street, Bedford.
Manned 08.00–23.00.

13 **Belfast** (NW) (Bill Thomson) Belfast 24635 & 24636.
The Samaritans, 67 Lisburn Road, Belfast BT9 7AE.

38 **Bexhill & Hastings** (SE) (Kathleen Burke) Hastings 666 & 6622.
The Samaritans, 29 Dorset Place, Hastings, TN34 1LG.
Manned 09.30–07.30.

25 **Birmingham** (WM) (David Evans) 021–643–2000 & 643–1411.
The Samaritans, 3 Brasshouse Passage, Broad Street, Birmingham B1 2HR.

105 **Blackburn** (NW) (Marjorie Fisher) Blackburn 61010 & 61525.

The Samaritans of North East Lancashire, 4 King Street, Blackburn, Lancs., BB2 2DH.

118 **Bognor Regis** (S) (Gerard Summergood) Bognor Regis 25555 & 25454.
The Samaritans, 13 Argyle Road, Bognor Regis, Sussex, PO21 1DY.

68 **Bolton** (NW) (Bill Evans) Bolton 21200 & 24394.
The Samaritans, 16 Bark Street, Bolton, Lancs., BL1 2BQ.
Manned 09.30–07.30.

BOSTON – Befriending group of Lincoln.

9 **Bournemouth** (S) (Roslyn Aish) Bournemouth 21999 & 28090.
The Samaritans, 1st Floor, Carrington, Wootton Gardens, Bournemouth, Hants.
Manned 09.00–22.00.

BRACKNELL – Befriending group of Reading (Hedley Ringrose) Bracknell 24055 & 24080.
The Pastoral Centre, Great Holland Square, Bracknell, Berks, RG12 4UX.
Manned 19.00–23.00.

15 **Bradford** (NE) (Dirk Bijl) Bradford 48585 & 48412.
The Samaritans, 21 Marlborough Road, Manningham, Bradford 8, Yorks.
Manned 10.00–22.00.

82 **Brent** (L) (Keith Johnson) 01–965–8000 & 01–965–8305.
The Brent Samaritans, 2 Tavistock Road, Harlesden. London, NW10.

94 **Bridgwater** (W) (Brian Whiting) Bridgwater 3388 & 2279.
The Samaritans, 18 Queen Street, Bridgwater, Somerset.
Manned 09.00–21.00.

BRIDLINGTON – Befriending group of Hull.

137 **Brierley Hill** (WM) (David Brown) 78111 & 78780.
The Samaritans, Hill Street, Brierley Hill, Staffs., DY5 2UE.

BRIGHTON – see Hove.

48 **Bristol** (W) (David Moseley) Bristol 298787 (3 lines).
The Samaritans, 37 St Nicholas Street, Bristol BS1 1TP.

BUDE – Befriending group of North Devon.

131 **Bury St Edmunds** (E) (William Wiseman) Bury St Edmunds 2345 & 62161.
The Samaritans, 16 Brentgovel Street, Bury St Edmunds, Suffolk.
Manned 09.00–23.00.

23 **Cambridge** (E) (Fred Wilkinson) Cambridge 54545 & 56420.
The Samaritans, 35 Regent Terrace, Cambridge, CB2 1AA.
Manned 09.00–24.00.

103 **Canterbury** (SE) (Ian Morris) Canterbury 60000 & 62035.
The Samaritans, 57 Ivy Lane, Canterbury, Kent.

72 **Cardiff** (W) (Kenneth Gillingham) Cardiff 30000 & 41459.
The Samaritans, 18 Park Grove, Cardiff, Glam.

112 **Carlisle** (NW) (Bert Longworth) Carlisle 28077 & 28053.
The Samaritans, 1a Fisher Street, Carlisle CA3 8RR.
Manned 14.00–16.00 & 17.30–23.00.

73 CENTRAL SCOTLAND (Scot) (Mary Dalziel) Falkirk 22066 & 22067.
Central Scotland Telephone Samaritans, 30 Newmarket Street, Falkirk, Stirlingshire.
Manned 09.00–22.00.

CHATHAM – see Medway Towns.

69 **Chelmsford** (E) (Albert Syson) Chelmsford 55111/2/3.
The Samaritans, 12 Critchett Terrace, Primrose Hill, Chelmsford, Essex, CM1 2QN.

39 **Cheltenham** (W) (Estelle Collin) Cheltenham 55777 & 54488.
Cheltenham & District Samaritans, 10 Royal Crescent, Cheltenham, Glos., GL50 3PE.

86 **Chester** (NW) (Drina Glyn-Jones) Chester 22999 & 25885.
The Samaritans, Talbot House, Lower Bridge Street, Chester, CH1 1RS.

CHESTERFIELD (NE) (John Kay) (attached to Sheffield).
Chesterfield 70000 & 75471.
Friendship House, Mount Zion Chapel, Chatsworth Road, Chesterfield.
Manned 14.00–07.00.

93 **Chilterns** (S) (Bob Stapleton) Amersham 5000 & 21223.
Chiltern Samaritans, 7 Hill Avenue, Amersham, Bucks.

47 **Colchester** (E) (Norman Abbott) Colchester 79999 & 76636.
The Colchester Samaritans, Markham's Buildings, Vineyard Street, Colchester, Essex CO2 7DG.

116 **Coleraine** (NW) (Brian Liddell and Tom Cunningham) Coleraine 4545 & 4546.
The Samaritans, 32a New Row, Coleraine, N. Ireland, BT52 1AF.
Manned 13.00–07.00.

125 **Cork** (W) (Jim Candon) Cork 021–21323.
11 Liberty Street, Cork, Ireland.

57 **Coventry** (WM) (Morritt Mayall) Coventry 22550 & 21540.
The Samaritans, 5a Priory Row, Coventry CV1 5EX.

CREDITON – Befriending group of Exeter.

54 **Crewe** (WM) (David Baker) Crewe 2144 & 3445.
The Samaritans of South Cheshire, 99 Edleston Road, Crewe, Cheshire.
Manned 09.30–12.30 & 19.00–22.00.

28 **Croydon** (L) (Cyril Franks) 01–681–6666/7.
The Samaritans, 2b Kidderminster Road, West Croydon CRO 2UE.

92 **Darlington** (NE) (Brenda Nicholson) Darlington 4444 & Bondgate 454.
The Samaritans, 2 South Arden Street, Darlington, Co. Durham, DL1 5RY.

8 **Derby** (WM) (Pat Tinniswood) Derby 40000 & 48993.

The Samaritans, 110 Burton Road, Derby DE1 1TG.
Manned 09.00–07.00.

33 **Doncaster** (NE) (Jim Latham) Doncaster 3636 &
65557.
The Samaritans, 36 Thorne Road, Doncaster, Yorks.
Manned 12.00–22.00.

117 **Dorset** (S) (Rex Page) Weymouth 71777 & 71778.
The Samaritans, Bank Buildings, South Parade
Entrance, Alexandra Gardens, Weymouth, Dorset.
Manned 10.00–22.00.

110 **Dublin** (NW) (Vincent Croggan) Dublin 778833.
The Samaritans, 66 South William Street, Dublin 2,
Ireland.

19 **Dundee** (Scot.) (George Brown) Dundee 26666 &
25678.
Dundee Telephone Samaritan Service, 28 South Tay
Street, Dundee.
Manned 09.00–23.00.

62 **Dunfermline** (Scot.) (Sheila Lyon) Dunfermline
22222 & 22271.
Telephone Samaritans, 16 Guildhall Street, Dunfermline.
Manned 14.00–22.30.

122 **Durham** (NE) (Gordon Roe) Durham 63737 &
63777.
Central Durham Samaritans, 26 Sutton Street,
Durham, DH1 4BW.

128 **Ealing** (L) (Raymond Bunce) 01–567–9977 &
01–567–3626.
The Samaritans, 4 Windsor Road, Ealing, W5.

63 **Eastbourne** (SE) (Ken Moore) Eastbourne 29933 & 24884.
The Samaritans, 30 Terminus Road, Eastbourne, Sussex, BN21 3LP.

53 **East Surrey & North Sussex** (SE) (Jim Woodward) Reigate 48444 & 48445.
The Samaritans of East Surrey & North Sussex, 42 Holmesdale Road, Reigate, Surrey, RH2 0BQ.

2 **Edinburgh** (Scot.) (Ian Walker) 031–225–3333/4/5.
Telephone Samaritans, 54 Frederick Street, Edinburgh, EH2 1LN.

141 **Elgin** (E. Simpson) Elgin 3000 & 2609.
The Samaritans, 5 High Street, Elgin, IV30 1EQ.

42 **Exeter** (W) (Tony Grimaldi) Exeter 77755 & 57572/3.
The Samaritans, 2 Wynards, Magdalen Street, Exeter, Devon, EX2 4HX.
FALKIRK – see Central Scotland.

43 **Folkestone** (SE) (Francis Capener) Folkestone 55000 & 57262.
The Samaritans, 65 Guildhall Street, Folkestone, Kent. CT20 1EJ.
Manned 10.00–20.00 Mon. to Sat.

4 **Glasgow** (Scot.) (Donald McMillan) City 4488 & 7922.
Telephone Samaritan Service, 218 West Regent Street, Glasgow C2.

121a **Gloucester** (W) (Jim Cottle) Gloucester 36333 & 32100.
The Samaritans, 1 Belgrave Road, Gloucester.
Manned 10.30–22.30.

GOOLE – Befriending group of Hull.

GRAVESEND – Befriending group of Medway Towns.

GREAT YARMOUTH (Associate Branch of Lowestoft) (J. Robinson) Great Yarmouth 2800.
1 Coronation Terrace, Regent Road, Great Yarmouth. Manned 18.30–22.00.

56 GRIMSBY (EM) (Mig Jary) Grimsby 54455 & 55835.
Grimsby, Cleethorpes & District Samaritans, 55 Alexandra Road, Grimsby, Lincs.
Manned 09.00–22.00.

30 **Guernsey** (S) (Bunny Crousaz) Guernsey 23030 & 23033.
The Samaritans, 42 The Bordage, Guernsey, C.I. (FOR CLIENTS' USE ONLY.)
Office Address: 'Greenlands', Rohais, St Peter Port, Guernsey; Guernsey 23380.
Manned 19.00–21.00.

34 **Guildford** (SE) (Elsie Sales) Guildford 72345 & 72346.
Telephone Samaritans, 69 Woodbridge Road, Guildford, Surrey.
Manned 09.00–23.00.

22 **Halifax** (NE) (Arnold Dawrant) Halifax 58585 & 62020.
The Samaritans, Warwick Chambers, 37 Southgate, Halifax, Yorks.
Manned 10.00–22.00 Mon. to Fri. and 10.00–13.00 Sat. and Sun.

136 **Hamilton** (Scot.) (David Redwood) Hamilton 29411 & 20604.
The Samaritans, 4 Selkirk Street, Hamilton, Lanarkshire, ML3 6RQ.

66   **Harrow** (L) (Mary Burrows) Harrow 7777 & 5079.
The Harrow Samaritans, 2 St John's Road, Harrow,
Mddx.

111   **Hartlepool** (NE) (Leon Heatley) Hartlepool 2929 &
66719.
The Samaritans, 122 York Road, Hartlepool,
TS26 9DE.

64   **Havering** (L) (Brian Mahood) Romford 40000 &
49339.
The Havering Samaritans, 107 North Street, Romford,
Essex, RM1 1ER.

135   **Hereford** (W) (Jerome Hodkinson) Hereford 69000
& 55570.
The Samaritans, 21 King Street, Hereford, HR4 9BX.

10   **Herts/Essex** (E) (Fred Pope) Ware 4099 & 4090.
The Samaritans, 68a High Street, Ware, Herts,
SG12 9DA.

138   **Hillingdon** (L) (Derek Strange) Uxbridge 53355 &
34216.
The Samaritans, Communicare, Redford Way,
Uxbridge, Mddx.

HITCHIN – see North Herts.

HONITON – Befriending group of Exeter.

140   **Horsham** (SE) (Douglas McDonald) Horsham
3455 & 4504.
The Samaritans, 13 Park Street, Horsham, Sussex.

99   **Hove** (SE) (Jake Webster) Brighton 733333 & 733409.
The Samaritans, 102 Clarendon Road, Hove, Sussex,
BN3 3WQ.

98 **Huddersfield** (NE) (Alan Spurr) Huddersfield 33388/9
& 28672.
The Samaritans, 28 St Peter's Street, Huddersfield,
Yorks.

14 **Hull** (NE) (Audrey O'Dell) Hull 23456 & 29477.
The Samaritans, 23 Waltham Street, Hull, Yorks,
HU1 3SL.

ILFORD – see Redbridge.

142 **Inverness** (Scot.) (Iain Taylor Campbell) Inverness
34000 & 31779.
The Samaritans, 5 Ness Place, Inverness, Scotland.

29 **Ipswich** (E) (Douglas Woolner) Ipswich 51000 &
58488.
The Samaritans, 9 Coytes Gardens, Ipswich, Suffolk,
IP1 1PS.
Manned 09.00–23.00.

ISLE OF WIGHT – see Portsmouth.

11 **Jersey** (S) (Fred Hodges) Central 30303 & 36880.
The Samaritans, 2 Hope Street, St Helier, Jersey, C.I.
Manned 10.00–22.00.

KILMARNOCK – see Ayrshire.

KING'S LYNN (David Kingcome) Associate Branch of
Norwich. King's Lynn 61616.
22 Queen Street, Kings Lynn.
Manned 10.30–22.30.

97 **Kingston on Thames** (L) (Frank Giles) 01–399–6660,
399–6676/7 & 01–390–0160.
The Samaritans, 12 St Andrew's Road, Surbiton,
Surrey, KT6 4TD.

KIRKCALDY – Befriending group of Dunfermline.

132 **Lancaster** (NW) (Paul Goodson) Lancaster 69696 & 69229.
The Samaritans, Y.M.C.A. Building, China Street, Lancaster.
Manned 9.00–22.00.

58 **Leatherhead** (SE) (Sam Muldoon) Leatherhead 75555 & 75556.
The Samaritans, 45 Lower Fairfield Road, Leatherhead, Surrey.

79 **Leeds** (NE) (Sheila Gledhill) Leeds 34567 & 39081.
The Samaritans of Leeds, 15 Kelso Road, Leeds, LS2 9PR.

65 **Leek** (WM) (Bernard Anwyl) Leek 4100 & 4527.
Leek & District Samaritans, Congregational School Rooms, Russell Street, Leek, Staffs.
Manned 09.00–23.00.

44 **Leicester** (EM) (Michael Charman) Leicester 700000 & 705330.
The Samaritans, 2 Elmfield Avenue, Leicester LE2 1RB.

100 **Lewisham** (L) (Yvonne Herbert) 01–692–2266 & 01–692–3330.
The Samaritans, 134–6 Lewisham Way, London SE14 6PD.

74 **Lincoln** (EM) (Robert Withers) Lincoln 23400 & 27788.
Lincoln & District Samaritans, 17 Hungate, Lincoln, LN1 1ES.
Manned 09.00–23.00; 14.00–20.00 (Sun.).

LIVERPOOL – see Merseyside.

1 **London** (L) (Chad Varah) 01–626–2277 for *all* calls (01–626–9000 also retained).
The Samaritans, 39 Walbrook, London EC4N 8BP.
The Samaritans, West End Annexe (John Eldrid), 24 Collingham Road, London SW5 0LX.
The Samaritans, East End Annexe, Greencoat School, Whitehorse Road, London E1.
SEE ALSO: Brent, Croydon, Ealing, Harrow, Havering, Hillingdon, Kingston, Lewisham, Orpington, Putney, Redbridge.

LOUTH – Befriending group of Grimsby.

120 **Lowestoft** (E) (Marion Courtney) Lowestoft 2800 & 63010.
Lowestoft Samaritans, 14 Beach Road, Lowestoft, Suffolk.

77 **Luton** (E) (David Clendon) Luton 20088 & 20933.
Luton Samaritans, 67 Adelaide Street, Luton, Beds.

80 MACCLESFIELD (NW) (Ian Nixon) Macclesfield 27000 & Greenhills 21037.
Telephone Samaritans, Townley Court, Macclesfield, Cheshire.
Manned 14.00–16.00; 19.00–23.00. At other times calls transferred to Manchester Branch.

7 **Manchester** (NW) (Robin Barsley) Blackfriars 9000 & 5228.
Telephone Samaritans, St Paul's Church, New Cross, Manchester M4 5EQ.

MANSFIELD – see North Notts.

76 **Medway Towns** (SE) (V. Wright) Medway 44846 & 42222.
The Samaritans, 42 Ross Street, Rochester, Kent.

3 **Merseyside** (NW) (Nancy Kerr) Liverpool 709–8888 & 709–2212.
The Samaritans of Merseyside, 34 Slater Street, Liverpool L1 4BX.

MIDDLESBROUGH – see Teesside.

NEWCASTLE – see Tyneside.

90 **Newport** (W) (Keith Oliver) Newport 59000 & 64293/4.
Newport & Monmouthshire Samaritans, 3 Waters Lane, Newport, Mon.

144 **Newry** (NW) (Matthew O'Hare & Malcolm Graham) Newry 2633.
1 Margaret Street, Newry, N. Ireland.

NORTHALLERTON – see North Riding.

95 **Northampton** (EM) (Peter Newman) Northampton 30266 & 39898.
The Samaritans, 15 Birchfield Road, Northampton NN1 5AW.

88 **North Devon** (W) (Fred Pennington) Barnstaple 4343 & 4290.
The North Devon Samaritans, 11 Tuly Street, Barnstaple, N. Devon.

143 **North Down** (NW) (John Turner) Bangor 63036/7.
The Samaritans, 92 Dufferin Avenue, Bangor, Co. Down.

NORTH HERTS. (Associate Branch of Luton) (Timothy Lewis-Lloyd) Hitchin 54433.
The Samaritans, 84d Tilehouse Street, Hitchin, Herts

126 **North Notts.** (EM) (Graham Thornton) Mansfield 31515 & 31516.
The Samaritans, 1a Grove Street, Mansfield, Notts., NG18 1EL.

59 NORTH RIDING (NE) (Percy Hartley) Northallerton 3030 & 3709.
The Samaritans, P.O. Box 10, Northallerton, Yorks. (FOR CLIENTS' USE ONLY.)
All correspondence: 4 Hutchinson Drive, Northallerton, Yorks.

21 **North Staffordshire** (WM) (Gordon Ravenscroft) Stoke-on-Trent 23555 & 23202.
North Staffordshire Samaritans, 3 Shelton New Road, Shelton, Stoke-on-Trent, Staffs., ST1 4PF.
Manned 10.30–08.00. 24 hours Sat. and Sun.

50 **North West Surrey** (SE) (Aidan Rossiter) Weybridge 44444 & 47622.
North West Surrey Samaritans, Samaritan Centre, Woburn Hill, Addlestone, Surrey, KT15 2QB.

78 NORTHWICH (NW) (Robert Westall) Northwich 3211 & 3212.
The Samaritans of Mid-Cheshire, 89 Witton Street, Northwich, Cheshire.
Manned 12.00–15.00, 19.00–22.00.
At other times calls transferred to Manchester.

46 **Norwich** (E) (Edward de las Casas) Norwich 28000 & 21161.
The Samaritans, 19 St Stephen's Square, Norwich NOR 71E.

18 **Nottingham** (EM) (Arthur Frymann) Nottingham 40506 & 46464.
Telephone Samaritans, 2a Standard Hill, Nottingham. NG1 6FX.

71 **Orpington** (L) (Ray Humby) Orpington 33000 & 29262.
The Samaritans, 9b Station Road, Orpington, Kent BR6 0RZ.

32 **Oxford** (S) (Patrick Parry-Okeden) Oxford 22122
The Oxford Samaritans, 9 Ship Street, Oxford OX1 3DA.

113 **Perth** (Scot.) (John Nicol). Perth 26666 & 27826.
The Samaritans, 5 Watergate, Perth.
Manned 09.00–23.00.

119 **Peterborough** (EM) (P. Cauwood) Peterborough 64848 & 65936.
Peterborough Samaritans, 78 New Road, Peterborough.

134 **Plymouth** (W) (Roy Harris) Plymouth 21666 & 21759.
32 Looe Street, Plymouth, Devon, PL4 0EA.

17 **Portsmouth** (S) (Sam Short) Portsmouth 65656 & 65657.
The Samaritans, 296 London Road, North End, Portsmouth, Hants., PO2 9JN.

109 **Preston** (NW) (Ada Forshaw) Preston 59000 & 59001.
The Samaritans, 11 St Wilfrid Street, Preston, Lancs., PR1 2US.

123 **Putney** (L) (Frank Himsworth) 01–789–8535 & 01–789–0544.
The Samaritans, 106 Felsham Road, Putney, SW15.

24 **Reading** (S) (Tony Fryer) Reading 54845 & 54846.
The Samaritans, Trinity Church Hall, Sidmouth Street, Reading RG1 4QX.

81 **Redbridge** (L) (P. Marshall) Ilford 2288 & 0890.
The Redbridge Samaritans, 2a Woodlands Road, Ilford, Essex.

REIGATE – see East Surrey & North Sussex.

RETFORD – Befriending group of Lincoln.

83 **Rochdale** (NW) (Sybil Other) Rochdale 31122 & 31181.
The Samaritans, The Champness Hall, Drake Street, Rochdale.
Manned 19.00–22.00. Manchester emergency number also advertised.

ROMFORD – see Havering.

26 **Salisbury** (S) (Philip Grubb) Salisbury 5522 & 27683.
The Salisbury Samaritans, St Martin's Church Street, Salisbury, Wilts.

SCARBOROUGH (associated Branch of Hull) (Audrey O'Dell) Scarborough 23456.
P.O. Box 999, Scarborough.

130 SCOTTISH CORRESPONDENCE BRANCH (D. S. C. Arthur).
The Samaritans, P.O. Box 9, Stirling, Scotland,
FK8 2SA.

49 **Scunthorpe** (EM) (Hugh Varah) Scunthorpe 60000 &
62757.
The North Lindsey Samaritans, 31 Dunstall Street,
Scunthorpe, Lincs.

61 **Sheffield** (NE) (Irene Waite) Sheffield 77277 &
26966.
The Sheffield Telephone Samaritans, 30 Rockingham
Lane, Sheffield.

SHEPPEY – Befriending group of Medway Towns.

51 SHREWSBURY (WM) (Betty Webb) Shrewsbury 4488 &
52401.
The Samaritans in Shropshire, 4a St Alkmund's Place,
Shrewsbury, Salop.
Manned 11.00–22.45.

SITTINGBOURNE – Befriending group of Medway
Towns.

102 **Slough** (S) (Philip Rogerson) Slough 31011 & 31012.
The Samaritans of Slough, 13 Bath Road, Slough,
Bucks.

35 **Southampton** (S) (Roy Chamberlain).
Southampton 32888/9 & 24466.
Telephone Samaritans, 64 St Andrew's Road, South-
ampton SO2 0BA.
Manned 10.00–07.00

75 **Southend-on-Sea** (E) (Bob Hann) Southend 42200
& 43739.

The Samaritans, 54 Hamlet Road, Southend-on-Sea, Essex, SS1 1NH.

40 STAFFORD (WM) (C. Heys) Stafford 2121 & 2271.
Stafford Samaritans, 15 Tipping Street, Stafford.
Manned 19.00–07.00; 15.00–07.00 (Sat. and Sun.)

STOCKTON – see Teesside.

STOKE-ON-TRENT – see North Staffordshire.

108 **Sunderland** (NE) (David Berg) Sunderland 77177 & 77427.
The Samaritans of Sunderland, 4 Vine Place, Sunderland.

16 **Swansea** (W) (Edward Hunt) Swansea 55999 & 52589.
The Samaritans, 60 Mansel Street, Swansea, Glam.

91 **Swindon** (S) (Keith Greenslade) Swindon 21445 & 27412.
The Samaritans Swindon & District Branch, Sanford Street Congregational Church, Swindon, Wilts.

96 **Teesside** (NE) Middlesborough 86777 & 85258.
The Samaritans of Teesside, Park Wesley Methodist Church, Linthorpe Road, Middlesbrough.

55 **Torbay** (W) (Malcolm Bell) Torquay 37171 & 25850.
The Samaritans, 21 Warren Road, Torquay, Devon.

114 **Truro** (W) (Tony Thorpe) Truro 6161.
The Samaritans, 19 Treyew Road, Truro, Cornwall.

85 **Tunbridge Wells** (SE) (Robert Whyte) Tunbridge Wells 32323 & 26771.

The Samaritans, 7 Lime Hill Road, Tunbridge Wells, Kent.

67 **Tyneside** (NE) (Ron Shuttleworth) Newcastle 27272 & 21523.
The Samaritans of Tyneside, 144 Westgate Road, Newcastle-upon-Tyne NE1 4AQ.
Manned 11.00–07.00.

124 **Wakefield** (NE) (Martha Williams) Wakefield 77011
The Samaritans of Wakefield & District, 41 George Street, Wakefield.

106 **Walsall** (WM) (Doris Hennessey) Walsall 24000 & 20000.
The Samaritans, Bott Lane, Walsall, Staffs.

WARE – see Herts/Essex.

104 WARRINGTON (NW) Warrington 38808 & 38809.
The Samaritans, St Clement's Mission, Bank Street, Warrington, Lancs.
Manned 19.00–23.00; Calls trans. 23.00–07.00; Calls trans. to Liverpool 07.00–19.00.

107 **Watford** (E) (Graham Ward) Watford 33333 & 32344.
The Samaritans, 2 Local Board Road, Watford, Herts. WD1 1LJ.

WEST DEVON – Befriending group of Exeter.

WESTON-SUPER-MARE – Befriending group of Bristol. 53 Oxford Street, Weston-super-Mare.

WEYBRIDGE – see North West Surrey.

WEYMOUTH – see Dorset.

84 **Whitehaven** (NW) (Bill Kerr) Whitehaven 4266 & 3370.
West Cumbria Samaritans, 102 Scotch Street, Whitehaven, Cumberland.
Manned 19.00–23.00 Mon to Fri. and 19.00–21.00 Sat.

127 WIGAN (NW) (Bob Metcalf) Wigan 44343 & 47303.
The Samaritans, 52 Market Street, Wigan, Lancs.
Manned 17.00–07.00. Calls trans. to Bolton outside these hours.

60 **Wolverhampton** (WM) (Malcolm McNicol) Wolverhampton 24515 & 25938.
Wolverhampton Telephone Samaritans, 24 School Street, Wolverhampton, WV1 4LF.

36 **Worcester** (WM) (H. Bill) Worcester 21121 & 28961.
The Samaritans, 20 The Tything, Worcester.
Manned 09.00–22.00.

101 **Worthing** (SE) (Ivor Balfour) Worthing 200000 & 35757.
The Samaritans, 4 Rivoli Buildings, Chapel Road, Worthing, Sussex, BN11 1BT.

129 **Yeovil** (S) (Howard Harrison) Yeovil 6455 & 3466
The Samaritans of Yeovil/Sherborne, 10 Everton Road, Yeovil, Somerset.

89 **York** (NE) (Norman Stainthorpe) York 55888 & 26952.
The Samaritans, 82 Bootham, York YO2 1QP.
Manned 10.00–07.00.

There are Preparatory Groups at Bangor (N. Wales), Enfield/Haringey (London), Nelson (Pendle), and Rhyl (N. Wales).

Emergency Telephone Services, encouraged by but independent of The Samaritans, in Universities and Colleges in Great Britain

ABERYSTWYTH (Nightline) Aberystwyth 4331/2.
Guild of Students, University College of Wales, Aberystwyth.

ALSAGER (Nite-Line) Internal 210.
Union Office, Cheshire College of Education, Alsager, Cheshire, ST7 2HL.

BATH (Nightline) Bath 5828.
Students' Union, Bath University, Claverton Down, Bath BA2 7AY.

BIRMINGHAM (Niteline) 021-472-4616 & 021-472-4741.
The Students' Union, Edgbaston, Birmingham, B15 2TU.

BRETTON HALL (Welfare Service) Int. 200 Ext. Bretton 238.
College of Education, Wakefield, Yorks.

BRISTOL (Education & Welfare).
University Union, Bristol.

BRUNEL (Nightline) 89-38349.
Brunel University Nightline, Uxbridge, Middlesex.

CAMBRIDGE (Link Line) 0223-67575.

17 St Edward's Passage, Cambridge.

CITY OF LONDON POLY (Nightline) 247–3388.
Students' Union, Fairholt House, Whitechapel Road, London E1.

EAST ANGLIA (Nightline) 0603–56161 Ext. 2242.
East Anglia University, Norwich.

ESSEX (Nightline) 0206–44144 Ext. 2345 Int. 156.
Essex University, Nr. Colchester, Essex.

EXETER (Nightline) 0392–75006/7.
Exeter University, Room 4, Devonshire House, Stocker Road, Exeter, Devon.

HERIOT-WATT (Nightline) 031–229–8111.
Heriot-Watt University, Edinburgh, Scotland.

HULL (Nightline) 0482–46367–9.
138 Cottingham Road, Hull.

ILKLEY (Nightline).
College of Education.

KEELE (Contact) 0782–71430.
University of North Staffs., Keele, Staffs.

LANCASTER (Nightline) 0524–65201 Ext. 4444.
Nightline, Lancaster University, Bailrigg, Lancaster.

LONDON (Nightline) 01–581–2468.
London University, Nightline, 8 Prince's Gardens, London SW17.

MANCHESTER (Contact Nightline) 061–273–1188/9.
161 Oxford Road, Manchester 13.

NOTTINGHAM (Nightline) 0602–57666 Int. 3400.
c/o Union Officer, Portland Building, University of Nottingham.

H*

OXFORD (Nightline) 0865-22122.
Oxford University Nightline, 2 Keble Road, Oxford.

ST ANDREWS (Nightline) St Andrews 2783.
University of St Andrews, Fife, Scotland.

SHEFFIELD (Nightline) 0742-79167.
Polytechnic, City College, and Totley College, Sheffield, Yorks.

SOUTHAMPTON (Nightline) 0703-58575.
The University, Southampton.

SURREY (Nightline) 0483-32710.
The University, Guildford, Surrey.

SWANSEA (Contact Nightline) Welfare Room 'phone.
Swansea University College, Glam., Wales.

TRENT (Nightline).
Trent Polytechnic, Soc. Welfare Committee, Students' Union, Shakespeare Street, Nottingham.

WARWICK (Nightline) 0203-69708 & 0203-24011 Ext. 2299.
Warwick University, Coventry, Warws.

YORK (Co-op) 0904-59861 Ext. 5999.
The University, York.

Overseas Branches of The Samaritans

BERMUDA – in preparation.

BLOEMFONTEIN – in preparation.

Bombay (Nadir Dinshaw; Sarah G. Dastoor) Bombay 397846.

The Samaritans, c/o Seva Niketan, Sir J. Jeejibhai Road, Byculla, Bombay 8, India.

The Samaritans, c/o Church of Our Lady of Perpetual Succour, Swami Vivekanand Road, Chembur, Bombay 71, India.

The Samaritans, c/o Afghan Church, Colaba, Bombay 5, India.

The Samaritans, Dev Kripa Mandai, M.M. Chotani Road, Mahim, Bombay 16, India.

BOSTON, Mass., U.S.A. – in preparation.

Bulawayo (C. E. Pilcher) Bulawayo 5000 & 5001.

The Samaritans, P.O. Box 806, Bulawayo, Rhodesia.

Calcutta (Vidayan Pavamani) Calcutta 442842.

The Samaritans, St Paul's Cathedral, Chowringhee, Calcutta 700016, India.

Overseas Branches of The Samaritans

Gdańsk (Tadeusz Kielanowski) Gdańsk 310000.
Anonymowu Przyjaciel, ul. Piwna 36, Gdańsk-Wrzeszcz,
Poland.

Hong Kong (Andrew Tu) Hong Kong 836611.
The Samaritans, Room 45, Block 13, G/F Lo Fu Ngam
Resettlement Estate, Kowloon, Hong Kong.

LISBON, Portugal – in preparation

PALMERSTON NORTH (J. Foote) P. North 74400 & 83942.
The Samaritans, 117 Park Road, Palmerston North, New
Zealand.
Manned 09.00–13.00; 17.00–23.00.

Perth (M. Levinson) Perth 811000 & 83501.
The Samaritans of Western Australia Inc., 86 Bagot Road,
Subiaco 6008, Western Australia.

Salisbury (M. Gear) Salisbury 22000 & 20201.
The Samaritans, P.O. Box UA 267, Union Avenue,
Salisbury, Rhodesia.

Saõ Paõlo (Jacques Conchon) 33.2050 & 36.6001.
Companha de Valorizacaõ da Vida, Rua Francisca Miquelina
323 c. 24, Bela Vista, Saõ Paõlo, Brazil.

Singapore (Gunnar Teilmann) Singapore 95644 & 65641.
The Samaritans, 254 Outram Road, Singapore 3.

TEHRAN, Iran – in preparation.

TRINIDAD – in preparation.

Umtali (R. H. Clark) Umtali 3559.
The Samaritans, 82 Second Street, Umtali, Rhodesia.
Manned 06.00–24.00.

Wellington (Walter Hurst) Wellington 49.600 & 49.601.
The Samaritan Telephone Service, P.O. Box 12044,
Wellington North, New Zealand.

Posts other than Branches of The Samaritans, affiliated to the International Federation of Telephone Emergency Services

The Samaritans believe that being open to any 'Samaritan-type' befriender, without regard to his religion, is of the essence of a non-medical suicide prevention service, and the 34 per cent reduction in the suicide rate of England and Wales since they became widespread would seem to support this belief. From their point of view, the freedom of a Centre from confessional control or bias is not a matter of taste or preference, but is crucial to the operation. Naturally, they do not deny the right of Churches to set up Centres for any legal purpose whatever, but they cannot, without betrayal of their own vocation, regard confessional Posts (or worse, rival confessional Posts in the same town) as having more than a superficial resemblance to them. Their own extensive recruitment of both lay and ordained Christians shows that they are not anti-religious, but they are accused of arrogance and intolerance when they state the fact that open and confessional Posts do not belong in the same organisation and the only honest reason for continuing to be so unequally yoked is in the hope that progress may be made towards openness, for the sake of the proven needs of the client.

The International Federation of Telephone Emergency Services arose out of the International Information Centre for Services of Emergency Telephonic Help set up at Geneva as a result of the conferences at Nyon (Switzerland) in 1960 and Bad Boll (Germany) in 1962.

The conflict between the open and the confessional Centres came to a head at Oxford in 1964 and continued at meetings of the International Committee until the conference at Brussels in 1967. Its sub-committee had drawn up International Norms similar to those on pp. 87–9, but even after emasculation they were vetoed by Sweden and Germany, whose representatives found themselves in an impossible position because of the sincere convictions which had led to the establishment of their Church-based services. It was no fault of theirs that they opposed, with the same honesty that the Samaritan representative insisted on, these Norms, and it is a mark of the progress that has been made that acceptance of almost identical Norms in 1973 was unanimous.

After much heart-searching The Samaritans, who felt that their whole ethos had been rejected, decided to continue what seemed then to be an unpromising dialogue. This was partly because of the sympathy and support of colleagues from Belgium, France, Italy and the Netherlands, and partly because of their confidence in the Rev. Rémi Mens, who was elected President of the newly formed Federation at Brussels in 1967. His re-election at Stockholm in 1970 led to the gradual acceptance of the need for openness which culminated in the successful 1973 Congress at Geneva, with 500 participants from 17 countries.

The new President of IFOTES, Bruno Burger, a layman

Other emergency telephone services affiliated to I.F.O.T.E.S.

with long experience of suicide prevention, has the task of seeing that the International Norms are applied everywhere by the time the 1976 Congress takes place – in Poland.

Note: To save space, addresses are not given, but postcode, town and name of service should ensure delivery of letters.

AUSTRIA

Two posts: one of Notrufdienst der Kath. und Evang. Kirche at 4020 Linz, 24355; one of Telefonseelsorge at 1010 Vienna, 639291.

BELGIUM

Six posts: five of Télé-Onthaal/Télé-Accueil at 2000 Antwerp (Rev. Rémi Mens, immediate Past President of the Federation), 03 379292; 1000 Brussels, 02 382808; 9000 Ghent, 09 239999; 7210 Cuesmes, 065 32020; 4000 Liège, 04 426565; one of Télé-SOS at 8400 Ostend, 059 78178.

CZECHOSLOVAKIA

Five posts: four of Linka Duvěry at Ostrava, ul Obdoje 1, Prague II, Ke Karlova 11, 297900; Pribram VII 159/2345; Trebic, 4444; one of Linka Nadeje at Brno 334455.

DENMARK

Six posts: five of Sct. Nicolai Tjenesten at 9000 Aalborg, 80011; 8000 Aarhus, 6126966; 1067 Copenhagen, 01121400; 6700 Esbjerg, 50011; 5200 Odense V, 90011; one of Die Offene Tür at 8200 Aarhus, 6165566.

FINLAND

Nineteen posts of Palveleva puhelin/Sjävårdstelefon at Helsinki 418033 (Finnish) 414135 (Swedish); Etelä-Karjala 34211; Hyvinkää 13477; Hämeenlinna 24652; Jyväskylä 19653; Jämsä 2670; Kemi 14400; Kouvola 18800; Lahti

Other emergency telephone services affiliated to I.F.O.T.E.S.

37100; Mikkeli 21600; Mänttä 47240; Oulu 16050; Pori 15566; Rovaniemi 10555; Savonlinna 22700; Seinäjoki 22222; Tampere 26600; Turku 27190; Vaasa 24188.

FRANCE

Twenty-two posts: 21 of SOS-Amitié France at Bordeaux 442222; Brest 802494; Clermont-Ferrand 935656; Dijon 323377; Grenoble 872222; Le Havre 463866; Lille 557777; Lyon 298888; Marseille 761010; Montpellier 630063; Nancy 529740; Nantes 734242; Nice 874874; Orléans 622222; Paris 8257050; Poitiers 417515; Reims 881010; Rennes 362525; Rouen 700715; St-Etienne 334399; Toulouse 808080; one of SOS-Téléphone at Strasbourg 343333.

GERMANY

Forty-five posts: 31 of Telefonseelsorge at 8580 Bayreuth, 5555; 1000 Berlin 12, 310236; 5300 Bonn-Bad Godesberg, 651616; Braunschweig, 333300; 2800 Bremen 1, 343030; 4600 Dortmund, 527070; 4000 Düsseldorf, 358888; 4300 Essen, II 224466; 2000 Hamburg 1, 335005; 3000 Hannover, 17766; 7500 Karlsruhe, 23366; 3500 Kassel-Wilhelmshöhe, 33240; 2300 Kiel, 47422; 5400 Koblenz, 34343; 5000 Köln, 318366; 4150 Krefeld, 750111; 2400 Lübeck, 78744; 6800 Mannheim, 22822; 8000 München 2, 595455; 8000 München, 530011; 4400 Münster, 40201; 8500 Nürnberg, 333500; 7000 Stuttgart 1, 223333; 7400 Tübingen, 4444; 8700 Würzburg, 53030; 5600 Wuppertal 2, 557766; four of Offene Tür at 1000 Berlin, 8817025; 2000 Hamburg, 325455; 3000 Hannover, 27161; 6800 Mannheim, 24680; two of Ruf & Rat at 4300 Essen, 224020; 7000 Stuttgart I, 622644; one of Beratungszentrum at 7000 Stuttgart, 294775; one of Evang. Telefonseelsorge at 6000 Frankfurt, 291015; one of Notruf-Telefonseelsorge at 6000 Frankfurt, 555536; one of

248

Other emergency telephone services affiliated to I.F.O.T.E.S.

Beratungsdienst Hauptwarch at 6000 Frankfurt, 292711-one of Seelsorgerliche Beratungs-strelle at 5000 Köln, 237723; one of Telefonseelsorge formerly Glaubens; information at 6500 Mainz, 20511; one of SOS Rat & Hilfe at 4020 Mettman, 24848; one of SOS-Telefonseelsorge-Notruf at 8000 München, 530011; one of Münchner Insel at 8000 München 220041; one of Rat & Hilfe at 4040 Neuss, 23535; and 4 additional posts of Telefonseelsorge at Darmstadt 22122, Pforzheim 14441, Regensburg 51313 and Wiesbaden 7070.

HUNGARY

Two Suicide Prevention Centres: one at Budapest, Vörös hds.-u. 116 (Dr Miklos Kun); and one at Debrecen, Museum u.4 (Dr Pal Szabo).

ITALY

Fifteen posts: twelve of Telefono Amico at Bologna 267891; Busto Arsizio 623331; 09100 Cagliari, 444941; Legnano 592211; 20121 Milano, 4384; 35100 Padova, 654566; Palermo 284200; 10121 Torino, 532053; 34100 Trieste, 766666; 33100 Udine, 58537; 21100 Varese, 289000; 30170 Venezia, 59900; 37100 Verona, 22990; two of Voce Amica at 39100 Bolzano, 25095; 50123 Firenze, 262639; one of SOS Voce Amica at 16100 Geneva, 595857 (the Post of Bruno Burger, President of I.F.O.T.E.S.).

NETHERLANDS

Sixteen posts of Telefonische Hulpdienst at Rotterdam, 365606; Amsterdam, 244444; Arnhem, 436000; Breda, 38450; Dordrecht, 32322; 'sGravenhage, 182266; Groningen, 250000; Haarlem, 326655; Heerlen, 716666; 'sHertogenbosch, 40048; Leeuwarden, 32000; Leiden, 25202; Nijmegen, 28280; Odijk, 1522; Venlo, 18888; Zaanstreek/Waterland, 62000.

Other emergency telephone services affiliated to I.F.O.T.E.S.

NORWAY
Four posts of Kirkens Natt-Tjeneste at Bergen, 211800; Oslo, 208635; Stavanger, 20430; and Trondheim, 20945.

POLAND
Six posts of Telefon Zaufania at Krakow, 37755; Lublin, 46100; Poznan, 58687; Torun, 00000; Warszawa, 274455; Wroclaw, 21717. Gdansk: see under Samaritans.

SWEDEN
Thirty-one posts: 28 of Jourhavande Pastor, all with tel. no. 90000, at 50242 Borås; Dalarna; Eskilstuna; 80001 Gävle; 41255 Göteborg; Gotland; 25262 Hälsingborg; 55257 Jönköping; 69100 Karlskoga; Katrineholm; 29100 Kristianstad; 58345 Linköping; Luleå; 21236 Malmö-Trelkborg; Nässjö (Rev. Åke Runmark); 60236 Norrköping; Örebro; Örnsköldsvik; Östersund; 81100 Sandviken; 54100 Skövde; 15132 Södertälje; 11440 Stockholm; 85250 Sundsvall; 46100 Trollhättan; 75321 Uppsala; 72590 Västerås; Växjö. Three posts of 'Service for Students' at Göteborg 135583; Stockholm 106920; Uppsala, 128704 (Gunnel Ceder).

SWITZERLAND
Eleven posts: 10 of Die Dargebotene Hand/La Main Tendue at 5000 Aarau, 228888; 3012 Berne, 231223; 2501 Bienne, 34545; 1211 Geneva 4, 250200; 1000 Lausanne, 322411; 6002 Lucerne, 237675; 9000 St Gallen, 231414; 7299 Seewis-Dorf, 521377; 8400 Winterthur, 291111; 8042 Zürich, 262020. One post of Telefono Amico at 6830 Chiasso, 48383.

Posts other than Branches of The Samaritans, not affiliated to the International Federation of Telephone Emergency Services

ARGENTINA

Buenos Aires, Centro de Asistencia al Suicida (Alfredo J. A. Gazzano).

AUSTRALIA

Several centres of Life Line, notably at 5000 Adelaide (Rose Hunt), 43 Franklin Street, tel. 51 5355 (Youth Line tel. 51 8280); and 3000 Melbourne (Arthur Preston), 148 Lonsdale Street, tel. 662 1000. Also at Brisbane, Sydney, etc. For Perth, Western Australia, see under Samaritans.

CANADA

BRITISH COLUMBIA

Campbell River Crisis Centre, 287–7471; Courtenay NOW, 334–2434; Nanaimo Crisis Centre, 754–4447/8; Prince George Crisis Intervention Line, 563–1214; Surrey Intersection, 596–1727; Trail Crisis Intervention Centre, 368–9114; Vancouver CRISIS INTERVENTION SUICIDE PREVENTION CENTRE, 733–4111; Victoria Cool-Aid, 383–1931; Victoria Need, 386–6323.

Other emergency telephone services not affiliated to I.F.O.T.E.S.

ONTARIO
Collingwood, Georgian Bay District Contact Centre, 445-0641; Kitchener-Waterloo Hi-Line, 884-2190; London Contact, 434-2121; Niagara Falls Telefriend Inc., 356-5566; Oshawa, Distress Centre, 576-1121; OTTAWA DISTRESS CENTRE, 238-3311; Pembroke Distress Centre, 735-0661; St Catherines Care-Line, 688-3211; Scarborough Distress Centre, 291-2111; Toronto DISTRESS CENTRE, 366-1121; Toronto DISTRESS CENTRE TWO, 486-1456; Windsor Tel-a-Friend, 252-3443.

QUEBEC
Montreal Tel-Aide, 935-1101; Quebec City Telaide, 522-1266.

NEW BRUNSWICK
Fredericton Chimo, 475-9464.

NEWFOUNDLAND
St John's Contact, 726-6153.

NOVA SCOTIA
Antigonish Rap-Line, 863-1212; Halifax Help-Line, 422-7444; Sydney Contact Line-Metrocenter, 539-1971.

ISRAEL
Jerusalem, Aran, c/o Mental Health Clinic, Beith Lehem Road.

JAPAN
Independent posts in Aizu-Wakamatsu, Kyoto, Osaka and Tokio.

KOREA
Seoul, South Korea, Agape House (Rev. Young-Min Lee), 24-329 Hwagokdong, Yongdungpo-gu.

Other emergency telephone services not affiliated to I.F.O.T.E.S.

MEXICO
Mexico City 6, A.M.A.D. (Jesus Callardo), Liverpool 25; tel. 464046.

NEW ZEALAND
NORTH ISLAND
Auckland, Samaritan Life Line. For Palmerston and Wellington, see under Samaritans

SOUTH ISLAND
Centres of Life Line at Christchurch, Dunedin and Nelson.

PAKISTAN
Peshawar, The Good Samaritans (James Magi Khan), 12 Sadar Road, Peshawar Cantonment, North West Frontier Province.

SOUTH AFRICA
Seven centres called Life Line, some of them under Life Line International, at Cape Town, Durban, East Rand, Goldfields, Kimberley, Pietermaritzburg and Witwatersrand.

SWEDEN
Lund, Kontakt-Tjänst (Ninnie Salmström), St. Södergatan 39, tel. (046) 11 0021.

U.S.A.
ALABAMA
Birmingham 323–7777; Decatur 355–8000; Florence 764–3431.

ARIZONA
Phoenix 258–6301; Tuscon 296–5411.

Other emergency telephone services not affiliated to **I.F.O.T.E.S.**

CALIFORNIA

Bakersfeill 325–1232; Berkeley North 849–2212, South 537–1323; Carmel 373–0713; China Lake 446–5531; Davis 756–5000; El Cajon 444–1194; El Toro 830–2522; Fresno 485–1432; Garden Grove 639–4673; Long Beach 435–7669; Los Angeles (Norman L. Farberow & Robert E. Litman) 381–5111; Orange 633–9393; Palm Springs 746–9502; Pasadena 798–0907; Sacramento 481–2233; San Anselmo 454–4524; San Bernardino 886–4889; San Diego 239–0325; San Francisco 221–1424; San Jose 287–2424; San Mateo (Charlotte P. Ross) 349–HOPE; San Rafael 454–4524; Stockton 466–2961; Vallejo 643–2555; Ventura 648–2444; Walnut Creek 939–3232.

COLORADO

Colorado Springs 471–4357; Denver 746–8485; Grand Junction 242–0577; Pueblo 544–1133.

CONNECTICUT

Bridgeport 336–3876.

DELAWARE

Dover 678–1225; New Castle 656–4428

DISTRICT OF COLUMBIA

Washington 629–5222.

FLORIDA

Gainesville 376–4444; Jacksonville 384–6488; Miami 649–8206, 379–2611; Rockledge 784–2433.

GEORGIA

Atlanta 572–2626.

HAWAII

Honolulu 521–4555.

Other emergency telephone services not affiliated to I.F.O.T.E.S.

ILLINOIS
Champaign 359–4141; Chicago 794–3609; Mt. Vernon 2421511; Peoria 691–7373; Quincey 222–1166; Watseka 432–5111.

INDIANA
Indianopolis 632–7575.

IOWA
Keokuk 524–3873.

KANSAS
Garden City 276–7689; Kansas City 371–7171; Wichita 268–8251.

LOUISIANA
Baton Rouge 388–8822.

MAINE
Bangor 947–6143; Brunswick 443–3300.

MARYLAND
Baltimore 367–7800.

MICHIGAN
Ann Arbor 761–9834; Detroit (Bruce L. Danto) 875–5466; Flint 235–5677; Holland 396–4317; Warren 758–6860; Ypsilanti 485–0440.

MINNESOTA
Minneapolis 330–7777; St. Paul 225–1515.

MISSISSIPPI
Meridian 693–1001.

MISSOURI
Kansas City 471–3000; St. Joseph 232–1655; St. Louis 388–2000.

Other emergency telephone services not affiliated to I.F.O.T.E.S.

MONTANA
Great Falls 453–6511.

NEBRASKA
Omaha 342–6290.

NEVADA
Reno 323–6111.

NEW HAMPSHIRE
Berlin 752–4431.

NEW JERSEY
Metuchen 549–6000; Plainfield 561–4800.

NEW MEXICO
Las Cruces 542–9241.

NEW YORK
Brooklyn 462–3322; Buffalo 854–1966; Ithaca 272–1616; New York 736–6191; Niagara Falls 285–3515; Rochester 275–4445; White Plains 949–0121.

NORTH CAROLINA
Durham 688–5504; Gastonia 867–6373; Greensboro 275–2852; Jacksonville 346–6292; Roanoke Rapids 537–2909; Sandford 776–5431.

NORTH DAKOTA
Bismarck 255–4124; Fargo 232–4357; Grand Forks 772–7258; Minot 838–5555.

OHIO
Akron 434–9144; Athens 592–3917; Canton 542–9811; Columbus 221–5445; Dayton 223–4777; Kent 672–4357; Newark 344–1111; Toledo 478–0361; Zanesville 452–8403.

OREGON
Corvallis 752–7030.

Other emergency telephone services not affiliated to I.F.O.T.E.S.

PENNSYLVANIA
Philadelphia 686–4420.

SOUTH CAROLINA
Greenville 239–1021.

TENNESSEE
Memphis 525–1717; Nashville 244–7444.

TEXAS
Abilene 673–3132; Amarilla 376–4251; Corpus Christi 883–6244; Dallas 521–5531; Fort Worth 336–3355; San Antonio 734–5726.

UTAH
Salt Lake City 484–8761.

VIRGINIA
Portsmouth 399–6393.

WASHINGTON
Bremerton 373–2402; Olympia 357–3681; Seattle 325–5550; Spokane 838–4428.

WEST VIRGINIA
Charleston 346–3332.

WISCONSIN
Eau Claire 834–5522; Elkhorn 245–5011; Madison 251–2345; Milwaukee 258–2040.

WYOMING
Cheyenne 634–4469.

The U.S.A. has also about 50 centres of Contact, part of Life Line International.

VIRGIN ISLANDS
St. Thomas, Hot Line, Box 696, St. Thomas, 00801 U.S.V.

YUGOSLAVIA
Split, Vruća Linija (Hot Line) (Peter Borun), Split, Dalmatia.

List of Contributors

Charles Bagg, M.A., M.R.C.S., L.R.C.P., M.R.C.Psych., D.P.M., Consultant Psychiatrist.

Ellen Balaszeskul, former Social Worker, Samaritan, West Berlin.

B. M. Barraclough, M.B., M.R.C.P., M.R.C.Psych., D.P.M., Consultant Psychiatrist.

Doreen Bromby, Samaritan.

George Day, M.A., M.D., Vice-Chairman, The Samaritans.

The Rev. John Eldrid, A.K.C., Deputy Director, The Samaritans, London Branch.

Richard Fox, M.B., B.S.(Lond.), M.R.C.P., M.R.C.Psych., D.P.M., Consultant Psychiatrist, Honorary Psychiatric Consultant, The Samaritans.

The Rev. Basil Higginson, M.A., General Secretary, The Samaritans.

H. Howitt, Coroner.

Alan H. B. Ingleby, O.B.E., B.Sc., Student Counsellor.

Norman Ingram-Smith, Founder/Warden, St Luke's

List of Contributors

H. J. Walton, M.D., Ph.D., F.R.C.P., F.R.C.Psych., D.P.M., Professor of Psychiatry, University of Edinburgh.

Dermot J. Ward, F.R.C.P., M.R.C.Psych., D.P.M., Consultant Psychiatrist.

Leila Waterhouse, A.R.C.M., Samaritan.

Editor

The Rev. Chad Varah, O.B.E., M.A., Founder of The Samaritans, Director of the London Branch, Chairman of the Overseas Committee.